The Toltec Civilization

An Enthralling Overview of the History of the Toltecs, Starting from the Classic Maya Period in Mesoamerica to the Rise of the Aztec Empire

Free limited time bonus

Stop for a moment. We have a free bonus set up for you. The problem is this: we forget 90% of everything that we read after 7 days. Crazy fact, right? Here's the solution: we've created a printable, 1-page pdf summary for this book that you're reading now. All you have to do to get your free pdf summary is to go to the following website:
https://livetolearn.lpages.co/enthrallinghistory/
Once you do, it will be intuitive. Enjoy, and thank you!

We forget 90% of everything that we've read in 7 days...

Get the free printable pdf summary of the book you've read AND much, much more... shhhh...

Enter Your Most Frequently Used Email to Get Started

DOWNLOAD FREE PDF SUMMARY

© Enthralling History

Contents

Introduction

The Toltec Empire was a pre-Columbian Mesoamerican civilization that flourished in the 10th and 11th centuries in central Mexico. The Toltecs arrived in central Mexico from the northern deserts and dominated the region because of their artisanship and tactile warfare. The Toltecs were so fierce and respectable that the Aztecs claimed to have descended from them. Whether or not this claim is true is a contested topic among historians. The Aztecs admired the Toltecs for their art, architecture, and culture, most of which the Aztecs adopted in their cities and towns. The Aztecs also adopted the Toltec language, Nahuatl, and in the Aztec society, the word for Toltec came to mean "artisan."

Most of what we know about the Toltecs today has been passed down to us through the Aztecs. These accounts are shrouded in myth and regard the Toltec empire as the apex of culture, sophistication, and civilization. Historicists believe the Aztec accounts of the Toltecs, drawing parallels to the corresponding archaeological evidence to support their claims. On the other hand, anti-historicists claim Aztec stories about the Toltecs cannot be taken at face value since they hinder actual research into the origin and culture of the Toltec civilization.

In the 6th century, the religious city of Teotihuacán was ravaged, and most of its major monuments were burned to the ground. Teotihuacán was the grandest and most distinguished city of Mesoamerica in the Classic Era. At its peak, Teotihuacán was a striking wonder of architecture and design with a soaring population of around 200,000. Historians today believe that the Toltecs either burned and destroyed the revered ancient city or, at least, had a hand in its destruction. The fact that the Toltecs rose from the ashes of Teotihuacán makes this proposition even more appealing. Today, we do not remember the Toltecs as great innovators like their neighbors, the Zapotecs, neither do we remember them as scientific and mathematical prodigies like the classic-age Mayans. We remember them as fearsome warriors who waged war in the name of religion. They established a permanent standing army with different warrior castes. Disciplined, skillful, and highly trained, the Toltec army used forts, garrisons, supply depots, and reserve units. They extended their power throughout the region, conquering several kingdoms, states, towns, villages, and settlements.

The Aztecs also revered the Toltecs for their capital city of Tula. The city was an urban center for the community with prominent pyramids and a large square. The largest pyramid in the city was known as *the Pyramid of Quetzalcoatl.* Quetzalcoatl, or *"the serpent of precious feathers,"* is a mythic figure worshipped by the Aztecs and other Mesoamerican cultures. Historians believe that one of the plazas in Tula could host around 100,000 people. They think it was probably used for festivals and big events. The city also had two ball courts where people would play a form of a ball game that was ubiquitous throughout the Mesoamerican region.

Figure 1: Central America

At the beginning of the 10th century, the Toltecs started encroaching on Mayan territory. Mayans had their share of big cities like Tikal and Chichen Itza, whose respective populations far exceeded that of Tula in its heyday. The semi-mythical king, Kukulcan, conquered the Mayan-controlled Yucatán Peninsula. There is a large temple in the city of Chichen Itza in the Yucatán Peninsula that was built in honor of Kukulcan. In addition to the Kukulcan temple, El Castillo, historians and archaeologists have noticed striking similarities between the Pyramid of Quetzalcoatl and the Temple of Warriors at Chichen Itza. Considering how the Mayans were already under the influence of Teotihuacán for a long time, it stands to reason that the Toltecs likely inherited that position from the Teotihuacán. With their vast-reaching empire, the Toltecs controlled one of the largest Mesoamerican empires in history for a little less than a century. From 1018 to 1025, a great famine took over the land resulting in the demise of the Toltecs. Over the next century, the Toltec authority diminished as civil wars, religious disputes, uprisings, and famines ravaged the land. In 1122, Tula burned to the ground.

Experts have been debating the role of the Toltecs for a long time. Some argue that the Aztecs exaggerated the myth of the Toltec civilization. Others claim that despite mythical events, the accounts of the Aztecs have the ring of truth to them. Unfortunately, the Aztec emperor Itzcoatl burned down historical codices and paintings, and later, the Spanish looted, plundered, and destroyed most relics and works of art. Today, we have a very narrow understanding of the Toltecs as compared to the Aztecs, the Maya, and other Mesoamerican civilizations.

In this book, we will delve into the history of the Toltecs, including the civilizations that preceded and followed them. To grasp the influence of the Toltecs on Mesoamerican life, one must understand what was happening before the Toltecs arrived, what changes they brought about, and how it affected life after them. We will dissect the relationship between the Maya and the Toltecs and try to understand how the Toltecs shaped the Aztec way of life. We will also discuss the arts, weaponry, social life, and mythical rulers of this glorious civilization. Moreover, we will discuss the different theories regarding their emergence in the early 10th century and their eventual demise in the 11th century.

PART 1: THE CLASSIC MAYAN ERA (250 BCE – 900 CE)

Chapter 1: The Great Mayan Cities

The Mayan civilization started developing in modern-day Guatemala, Belize, southeastern Mexico, west Honduras, and west El Salvador around 2000 BCE. This era is referred to as the Preclassic Period of the Maya – it continues up to 250. The Maya were not a common people but a collection of disparate settlements with similar cultures that developed in tandem with each other. The word "Maya" is used today largely as an umbrella term. These settlements did not call themselves Maya, nor did they identify themselves as a cohesive unit.

The first true civilization to appear in the Preclassic period was the Olmec. The Olmecs appeared around 1200 BCE in the modern-day tropical lowlands of the Gulf of Mexico. The major Mayan cities of Tikal, Calakmul, and Copán would develop to its southeast and carry the notable influence of the Olmec culture. The Olmecs were discovered by large sculptures of carved stone depicting their heads. Seventeen of these helmet-wearing heads have survived down the centuries. Four of those seventeen were found in the capital city La Venta, which was the cultural hub of the Olmec. The complex and developed architecture implies that it served as a center for the Olmec state. Nevertheless, the earliest known Olmec center was San

Lorenzo. It was not until the decline of San Lorenzo that La Venta became the major center of Olmec activity.

In the Middle Preclassic Period – from 1000 BCE to 400 BCE – small villages grew and formed cities. In the Late Preclassic Period – ranging from 400 BCE-250 CE – large cities started appearing on the map. Several cities sprouted up in Petén Basin, a region located in southeastern Mexico and northern Guatemala. The city of El Mirador in Petén is widely regarded as one of the first capital cities of the Mayan civilization. Although the city had been around since the 6th century BCE, it reached its zenith in the 3rd century BCE. Another site that dominated through the Middle Preclassic Era was Nakbe that was closely connected to El Mirador. The Guatemalan Highlands, located in the south of Guatemala, was also home to different cities. One of the major cities of this region was Kaminaljuyu. After studying the remains, archaeologists think the Mayans created it before the end of the Preclassic Era in 250. Urban developments in nearby areas have hindered the ability of experts to estimate the size, scale, and political and economic significance of the city.

The Mayan civilization extended from 7000 BCE to 1524 CE, but it started to unlock its true potential in the 3rd century. The exponential evolution of the Mayan civilization started around 250, marking the beginning of the Classic Period of the Mayas. In the Classic Period, the Mayans developed a penchant for artistic and intellectual pursuits. They started to engage in large-level construction and started establishing large cities. Full of monumental architecture, sculpture, and art, these cities often contained 5,000 to 50,000 inhabitants. The greatest of these Mayan cities was Tikal, also known by its older name, *"Yax Mutal."* The city had been around since 300 BCE, but it truly came into its own after the collapse of the Preclassic period in which major cities like El Mirador and Kaminaljuyu were deserted and severely depopulated. The population of Tikal began to grow in the Preclassic Period and continued to grow rapidly through the Classic Period.

Figure 2: Tikal

While Tikal was finding its footing in the Early Classic Period, another city appeared in the Valley of Mexico known as Teotihuacán. The initial settlements in the area date as far back as the 6th century BCE. The settlements did not evolve into an urban phenomenon until the 2nd century BCE, when farmers working on the hillside started to migrate into the valley. In the 1st century BCE, Teotihuacán was turnings into a metropolitan unlike any other in Mesoamerica. From the 1st century to the 4th century, the city underwent a period of massive expansion and progress. From 350 to 650, the city witnessed its peak era, also known as the classical period of the Teotihuacán. During this time, the city's population skyrocketed to around 125,000, making it one of the biggest cities of the ancient world. Historians assume that the most imposing factor of the city's attraction was the religious sentiments attached to it. With great power comes great influence, and Teotihuacán was no exception to this rule. As the might of the city increased, it started influencing neighborly states and regions, including Tikal. Its influence might have extended to the city of Chichen Itza in the north.

The Maya capitals were usually surrounded by smaller cities that contributed to the wealth and prosperity of the entire kingdom. The kings preferred to work from and live in these capitals because of their proximity to other cities and their vast strategic relevance. Tikal was surrounded by many Maya cities and settlements, and Tikal's relationship with these states often varied. Inscriptions detail relations with Uaxactun, Caracol, Naranjo, and especially Calakmul, with whom Tikal would go on to develop a fierce rivalry. But Tikal was a big city, and even though it had its share of squabbles with nearby states, it had also developed relations with faraway cities like Teotihuacán. Records show that Teotihuacán had embassies in Tikal in the 1st century, but it was not until the 4th century that the dealings between the two cities intensified.

In 378, Tikal came into direct contact with Teotihuacán – we do not know whether it was in the form of a direct invasion or intervention via puppet rulers, but from this point onward, we find that the foreigners exert a substantial impact on the arts, culture, rituals, and other social practices in Tikal. Under the hegemony of Teotihuacán, Tikal began to expand. In the 4th century BCE, Tikal conquered Uaxactun and allied with Kaminaljuyu, increasing its access to the major trade routes in the region. In 426, Tikal's ever-expansive regime also enveloped Copán, an agricultural site that had become a city of obvious geographical importance. In the same year, the Tikal-Copán alliance founded the site of Quiriguá near Copan. Tikal sponsored the dynastic rise of Copán, and the remains of the site imply characteristics of Teotihuacán.

Around this time, another city named Calakmul was at the forefront of Mayan glory. Calakmul was a major state in the north of the Petén region that had access to trade networks with cities like El Mirador, Nakbe, and El Tintal. The city dates to the Preclassic Period, but it turned into a major Maya power in the Classic Era. Tikal and Calakmul were superpowers in their own right – and as is the case with superpowers, only one could come out on top. Hence began an immense competition and rivalry between the two city-states. Both cities established their networks of allied cities and engaged in a series of wars known as the Tikal-Calakmul Wars.

550 marks the beginning of the Late Classic Era of the Mayan civilization. Researchers estimate Calakmul's peak population in this era reached 50,000, and its authority over land extended as far as 150 km; it covered an area of roughly 70 square km. Much like Tikal, Calakmul had secondary cities around it that contributed to its growth and population. The cities of Naachtun, Oxpemul, Uxul, Sasilha, and La Muñeca had a combined population of around 200,000. Despite all this, Calakmul was the inferior city since the grandiose Tikal was home to around half a million people at the time. The first war ran its course from 537 to 572. Calakmul conquered a major city called Yaxchilan and continued to ally itself with states that were against the rule of Tikal. In 562, Tikal won a short-lived victory in the city-state of Caracol, an ally of Calakmul. But it was not to be as Caracol and Calakmul soon turned the tables and defeated Tikal. This initiated a long hibernation period for Tikal, also known as the "Tikal hiatus," during which the city went through a major lapse in urban and commercial progression.

Tikal's influence in the region plummeted, and the opposing forces may have forcibly removed most of its population. In the following years, Calakmul gained the upper hand in the region, but not for long. Tikal's influence had lessened, but it had not diminished. Over the next 100 years, Tikal and Calakmul engaged in a cold war. Tikal continued to defeat its local rivals, some of whom had helped Calakmul in the first war.

In 629, Tikal founded a military outpost, Dos Pilas, to control trade routes along the Pasión River located in the northern lowlands of Guatemala. In 648, Dos Pilas aligned with Calakmul, started a proxy-war against Tikal, and consequently gave rise to the Second War between the two Mayan superpowers. In 672, Tikal attacked and captured Dos Pilas. The exiled leader of Dos Pilas retaliated and captured a Tikal lord in 679, giving Calakmul a temporary foothold in the region. From 692 to 695, Calakmul dominated Tikal when by a twist of fate, Tikal turned the tables by winning a major battle against

Calakmul. The war continued until 705, when Tikal was defeated once again and Dos Pilas started to come into its own.

In the meantime, the city of Teotihuacán witnessed a major decline. Initially, archaeologists thought that invaders razed and burnt it to the ground. However, historians in recent times have pointed out that the burning was restricted to elite structures, hypothesizing that the city might have gone through a class conflict that resulted in a violent uprising. This theory carries a lot of weight as the timeframe coincides with the extreme climate change in the Northern Hemisphere in 535 and 536. Several other Mayan cities will undergo the same fate in the Classic Maya Collapse of the 8th and 9th centuries. From the ashes of Teotihuacán rose the Toltec empire, but we will get to that in due time.

Even after the fall of Teotihuacán, Tikal continued its tradition of impressive architecture and culture, but things were not looking well on other fronts. Quiriguá, which existed as an extension and a vassal of Copán, declared independence and shifted its allegiance to Calakmul in 738. This era marks the Third War between the two city-states. Copán wanted to retaliate against the smaller state but was probably afraid of Calakmul's military intervention. In one fell swoop, Calakmul managed to weaken an ally of Tikal and gained a small vassal state in return. The terms favored Quiriguá as well because it was quite far away from Calakmul and did not have to fear a complete usurpation. Tikal took over two major allies of Calakmul, El Peru, and Naranjo, in 743 and 744, respectively. Calakmul's influence in the region waned significantly as it lost control of its extensive trade network, vassals, and allies. Despite having emerged victorious, Tikal was in bad shape as well.

In the mid-8th century, we arrive at the Classic Maya collapse, also known as the Terminal Classic Era of the Mayans. In this period, populations started to decrease throughout the land, and major cities were deserted. Cities like Copán, Tikal, and Calakmul went into decline, both economically and politically. Archaeologists notice a decrease in large-scale architectural construction during this period and a cessation of inscriptions detailing crucial events. This sudden collapse is a strange archaeological mystery that is yet to be solved. The last record of a reign in Copán refers to 763. Similarly, monuments were raised in Calakmul in 790, 800, and 810, but little activity is recorded after that. From this point onward, the state's vassals started to erect their monuments, signaling a relocation of population and authority. Several theories exist to explain the collapse of the Mayan civilization, including epidemics, droughts, foreign invasions, internal religious and political squabbles, uprisings, and ecological collapse. All these theories try to understand how the collapse came about, but it is important to note that the Maya continued to exist and even flourish after their Classic Era. However, the civilization returned to numerous highs over the years, the glory of the Classic Era never returned.

After reading about a "lost city" in the writings of John Lloyd Stephens and his illustrator Frederick Catherwood, the commissioner and the governor of Petén visited the site of Tikal in the mid-19th century. It soon became a center of interest for archaeologists around the world. Nevertheless, it was not a discovery for the locals residing alongside the ancient city for centuries. Today, the Tikal site consists of approximately 3000 structures, including tall temples, nine plazas and courts, palaces, a market complex, ten reservoirs, and a unique ball court, all connected by causeways. Looking at Tikal and other Maya cities of the ancient world, we realize that the cities span outward – haphazardly and without a grid structure. By studying their location, it is clear that major cities were positioned to aid trade and provide benefits of a tactile nature. Cities with favorable food production and trade routes would naturally expand into capital states.

Chapter 2: Mayan Social Life and Economy

As discussed before, historians categorize ancient Mayan life into three major epochs: the Preclassic Period, the Classic Period, and the Postclassic Period. The Preclassic Period extends from 2000 BCE to 250 CE and charts the rise of the Mayan empire from humble settlements to magnanimous metropolitans. It is unclear how long the Mayans had inhabited the Mesoamerican land, but we do know that before 2000 BCE, the Mayans were purely hunters. Somewhere around the 2000 BCE mark, they introduced an agrarian element to their hunter-gatherer lifestyle. One of the first crops they learned to grow was corn, which soon became the staple crop of the region. They also learned to farm beans, chilies, tomatoes, squash, and cocoa during the Preclassic Period. Evidence suggests that cocoa may have been used as an alcoholic beverage since the 15th century BCE. Despite cultivating food, their diet mainly consisted of gathered edibles and meat from fish and land animals.

The Olmecs were the first to develop a system of writing, although it was not as legible or complete as the later scripts and hieroglyphics in Mayan chronology. They also developed urban environments with different rituals and practices like ballgames, chocolate drinking, and jaguar worship. They envied jade and developed trade routes across the land to obtain it. This trade network connected different regions and states and would keep expanding through the Classic Period. Trade routes also help spread the cultural features of the Olmecs throughout Mesoamerica.

From the 10th century BCE to the 4th century BCE, agricultural life became increasingly complex. Canals and irrigation systems that required coordinated human effort started appearing. The Olmecs erected statues and monuments, constructed causeways, and adopted corn as a crucial diet component. At the end of the Preclassic Period, the states of Kaminaljuyu and El Mirador emerged, and the Mayan way of life started to take form.

In the Classic Period, the Maya established an agricultural base for their economy. In Mesoamerica, agriculture used to be and still is a challenging endeavor. The condition of the soil is unsavory, and there is an apparent lack of usable land. In any case, agriculture is a risky venture anywhere in the world, and throughout history, various civilizations have applied different techniques to alleviate the risks. For instance, in medieval times, European farmers used scattered strips of land to alleviate risks and make up for potential losses. Most Mesoamerican civilizations countered this issue by switching between different strips of land during various seasons, allowing them to adapt to the low-nutrient soil. The Maya, like the Olmecs before them and the Aztecs after them, cultivated corn, beans, and squash in conjunction. The corn sucks nitrogen out of the soil, and the beans help rejuvenate it. Some historians hint at soil erosion as one of the major causes for the collapse of Teotihuacán. To avoid falling prey to this catastrophe, the Maya grew most of their food products in forest gardens known as "pet kot." The Maya created raised fields and terraces – large sections of receding flatlands on a sloped plane. The Maya connected raised fields by canals, giving birth to a sophisticated irrigation system on farming lands. Terracing with proper irrigation prevents the depletion of nutrients. The Mayan diet consisted primarily of corn, fish, honey, beans, turkey, vegetables, and chocolate drinks. In addition to agriculture, they obtained food from foraging and hunting.

Despite having grown with squash and beans, maize was the signature crop. The Mayan story of human creation talks about gods who created humans from yellow and white corn. These ideas were in keeping with the pantheon of animal gods that the Olmecs worshipped. The ceremonial centers, temples, pyramids, and plazas emphasize the rigorous religious sentiment in Mayan communities. The construction of stone structures, mostly religious ones, was a source of attraction and often contributed to the appeal of a metropolitan. The city of Teotihuacán started as a religious center and then turned into one of the biggest cities in Mesoamerican history.

The advent of urban centers allowed the Mayans to make serious headway in the fields of mathematics and astronomy. They invented the concept of zero: a representation of a non-entity that helped them solve difficult problems. They created a complex calendar that facilitated agricultural produce over multiple cycles. The Mayans also developed a sophisticated writing system that was far more comprehensive than the Olmec one. They used the inner bark of fig trees to make paper and wrote hieroglyphs in extensive codices. They had inherited their love of sculpture from the Olmecs and fondly inscribed on stone and reliefs. Most of what we know about the Mayans comes from these hieroglyphic accounts on pottery, stone slabs, and structures. These accounts reveal that while Mayans were mostly farmers, they had their fair share of violence and conflict as well. Uprisings were quite common, and city-states often engaged in battles to usurp control of the region.

As far back as the Preclassic Era, the Mayan society had a radical divide between the elite and commoners. With time, the Mayan society became more complex and sophisticated by specialization and division of labor. These distinctions also streamlined the political and social hegemony. As small rural communities turned into small cities and small cities turned into staples of dazzling architecture and culture, the interaction of political and prestigious classes blossomed into a unique nexus. The wealthy factions turned into clans and nobilities. The Maya aristocracy resided in the cultural hub. One would find the most profound and extraordinary artistic statements in this area: glamorous buildings, divine inscriptions, and beautiful sculptures.

The highest authority belonged to the king and court. The king used to be the ultimate supreme leader – a semi-divine figure worthy of mythical lore. The king acted as the middle ground between the realm of the mortals and the realm of the gods, and the masses often identified him with the maize god. The idea gains more credibility when one looks at the semi-mythical emperor Kukulcan who eventually became the feathered serpent god in the religion and mythology of the Yucatec Maya. Kukulcan is sometimes associated with the Aztec god Quetzalcoatl, and some historians believe that the two are the same deity.

The Maya civilization was a patrilineal society, meaning that the power passed from a king to his son. Typically, the eldest son would take over the king's duties, but this was not always the case. The successor had to meet certain criteria to ascend to the throne. The potential king must have possessed great military and tactical skills since the unstable Mayan terrain often called for kings to engage in battles. The coronation of the new king usually calls for a highly sophisticated ceremony – in this respect, the Maya were not different. The kings inaugurated their reign by sitting on a jaguar-skin cushion, holding a scepter, and wearing a jade headband and a headdress made of quetzal feathers. A king would bypass his son in favor of his queen if the sanctity of the nation were at stake. Quite similar to modern times, the transition of power needed to be peaceful, and the king and the nobility would elaborate before making a decision.

Not based on a bureaucratic or even a democratic model, the Mayan political structure was purely hierarchical. Different polities formed different royal courts, each catering to its own needs. Noble titles were restricted to these royal courts and the aristocracy. The aristocrats usually sponsored the court officials, and while all these nobles had a considerable say in the matters of state, the most notable authority was that of the "divine lord." Nevertheless, the sociological and political impact of the aristocracy increased as the Maya population witnessed significant growth from the Early and Middle Classic Periods to the Late Classic Period. With expansion and diversification, especially during the Classic Era, other factions like the priesthood and warrior classes also rose to prominence. Differences between these various classes often led to compromises – dynamic political institutions were formed to alleviate the situation, and disagreements were resolved in public settings where the Maya performed their usual rituals of dance and human sacrifice.

By the Late Classic Era, the title of the divine lord had lost some of its prestige. The Maya referred to the members of the ruling class as "ajaw" and the divine lord as the "k'uhul ajaw." The hieroglyphic inscriptions associate ajaw and other royal titleholders with certain city structures. Another title for the royal bloodline was "kalomte," but that was given only to the most formidable and commanding emperors. The kalomte would command the ajaw who, in turn, commanded "sajal," an official in charge of a small site of military importance. A sajal could be a regional governor or a war captain in charge of prisoners of war.

Like any society, the largest sector of the population comprised of commoners who made up around ninety percent of the entire Mayan population. The commoners formed the backbone of the Mayan economy. They cultivated various edible foods, engaged in trade and commerce across different cities, interacted with each other in marketplaces in big cities, and created some of the most unique luxury items and jewelry. Yet, very little is known about them. There are little to no remains of civilian houses – time, natural catastrophes, and ecological damage have had their way to them. The king, nobility, and aristocracy bankrolled artists and other individuals of cultural importance. Anyone who was not of noble birth was considered a commoner, so it is unsurprising that they do not feature in the inscriptions, hieroglyphs, or artwork.

The major source of Mayan economic activity was agriculture, raw goods, and trade. They used to extract raw materials like jade, wood, gold, and copper from the terrain. They used these and other raw materials to manufacture clothing, weapons, paper, furniture, codices, and luxury items. The artisans and workers made up a strong middle class that produced commodities and exotic goods. The most valued commodities were salt as it helped in the preservation of food, cocoa since the Maya were fond of drinking it and valued it immensely, and metals like jade and obsidian for their obvious economic value. The most skilled mathematicians, artists, and artisans would bypass this chain of command and sell their services separately. The Maya relied on the knowledge of astronomers, architects, scribes, sculptors, artists, mathematicians, and farming experts. They even had a service sector where experts in specialized fields would sell their services.

An educated merchant governor used to direct regional trade by assessing the production and supply of the goods. Atop the middle-class structure sat advisors of varying knowledge and skill. The advisory board was responsible for maintaining trade and, consequently, stable relations between different states. By ensuring supervision across all strands of the middle and lower classes, the Maya had developed a highly urbanized society with varying modes of integration.

The small towns kept to themselves, rarely engaging in long-distance trade – if ever –, relying heavily on the local exchange. Even the most efficient and capable households depended on local exchange for essential items. With time, smaller settlements began to specialize in specific goods and services. In the Classic Period, the cities grew tenfold, and trade between different cities and realms became quite common, providing a boost to the smaller villages and towns. Smaller villages became a part of the trade routes, and as such, started to witness more activity. Traders needed to stop and rest, and small villages provided a welcome change from the harshness of the routes. This helped invigorate the economy of small towns, and the Mayan society soon turned into a highly integrated trading empire.

The Maya used a basic barter system for the exchange of goods. During the Postclassic Era, cocoa beans were widely used in everyday deals. Since most Mesoamerican civilizations valued jade, gold, and copper highly, they were utilized for expensive purchases and large orders. As the Maya lifestyle based on local and foreign exchange gained traction, the trading network extended beyond Mayan territory and throughout all of Mesoamerica.

Chapter 3: Great Monuments of the Maya

A mere glance at Tikal serves as a gentle reminder of how architecturally advanced the Mayans were. After defeating the neighboring state of Calakmul, the people of Tikal ushered into a prolific period of planning and building gigantic structures and astonishing monuments. During this time, the city's inhabitants erected Temples I and II. Like most Mayan cities, the inhabitants of Tikal abandoned their ascending pyramids and statuesque structures after the decline. Over the years, the forests hid the foundations of these structures underneath their quiet shelter, away from prying eyes. In 1839, John Lloyd Stephens, accompanied by Frederick Catherwood, arrived in Central America. Passing through a harsh landscape – thanks to civil war, political instability, and strife – they finally arrived at a marvelous carved stone slab. As they proceeded with their expedition in and around the area, they stumbled upon more stairways, agricultural terraces, and stone walls. It caught the interest of various scholars, and several researchers and travelers started traveling to Central America.

The remains of Tikal boast more than 3000 structures, including enormous palaces and soaring temples connected by causeways. The structures were erected with the extensive use of limestone, and their design depicts the influence of Teotihuacán. The city also housed ball courts for playing Mesoamerican ballgame, smaller pyramids, platforms, stone monuments, administrative buildings, a market complex, reservoirs, and residences. The large structures portray the trademark features of Maya art and architecture: stepped pyramids, raised platforms, and long staircases accompanied by vaulted chambers and images of gods. The Great Plaza lies in the middle of the city, shielded by a temple on the east and another on the west. The North and Central Acropolis feature on the other two sides of the plaza. Built approximately in the 4th century, the Great Plaza and the North Acropolis have captured the imagination of researchers for quite a long time. A major reason for the scholarly interest is the navigational complexity of the two structures. Both the Great Plaza and the North Acropolis were built along a north-south axis, serving as evidence of the Maya's acclaimed knowledge of astronomy. Contrary to these two structures, Temples I and II, built in the Late Classic Era, stand across an east-west axis. The temples stood at impressive heights of 47 and 38 meters, respectively.

Temples I and II are just two temples in a group of six prominent pyramids with temples. The pyramids, titled Temples I-VI, all feature at least one large stairway and contain temples on their respective summits. These six temples were erected in the 8th and 9th centuries. The roof comb of Temple I was adorned with a giant sculpture of a Maya king. The temple contained a large collection of inscribed objects such as bone tubes and strips depicting humans as well as the ancient Mayan deities. The site also had jade ornaments and ceramic vessels. The doorways of Temples I and II are spanned by partially carved wooden lintels. The Temple III, known as the "Temple of the Jaguar Priest," has a height of 55 meters and boasts drawings of deities and rituals. Temple IV is the tallest structure of the family and stands at a whopping height of 70 meters. Although a couple of other structures may have been taller in their heyday, it is the largest existing Mayan structure and the second-largest existing pre-Columbian structure in the New World. Fifty-seven meters tall, Temple V is the second largest structure of Tikal. Finally, Temple VI stands at a modest 12 meters and is known as the "Temple of the Inscriptions" on account of having a lengthy hieroglyphic text on the back and sides of its roof comb. The hieroglyphics narrate the history of Tikal, starting from Preclassic Times in 1139 BCE.

All the great Mayan rulers dwelled in the five-story royal palace in the Great Plaza. It has enclosed courtyards for bloodletting and sacrificial ceremonies as well as spacious galleries. The North Acropolis contains temples built on two flat surfaces. It served as a funerary complex and as a burial ground for the nobility. The structure was vertically extended, and additional temples were added on top of the old structure for every subsequent royal burial. Just like the North Acropolis, there is also a South Acropolis to the southwest of the Great Plaza. To the west of the South Acropolis lie the architectural group of "Mundo Perdido," or the "lost world." The Mundo Perdido is situated alongside the Plaza of the Seven Temples and is home to the largest ceremonial complex in the entire city. Embellished with stucco masks of the Sun god, the Lost World Pyramid is the largest in Mundo Perdido and was probably built in the Late Preclassic times. The complex dates to the Preclassic Era and has been reconstructed many times.

As much as the glorious structures of the ancient Maya seduce us today, the tale of the ancient Maya was much more alluring before John Lloyd Stephens stumbled upon the ancient ruins in the 19th century. The Mayan legend fascinated scientists, archaeologists, and historians for centuries. The daring individuals who ventured into Central America in search of Mayan relics and lost cities had to rely on, more than anything else, sheer luck. It was difficult to approach the area with adequate preparation and knowledge because the Western world had just heard myths and stories. Although the Mayan civilization was merely a curiosity for the North Americans and Europeans, it was an absolute material reality for the local populations of Central and South America. Various populations in Guatemala, Belize, Peru, and Mexico had been living alongside these ruins for centuries. For them, the tall structures sticking out of canopies and forests were not the remnants of a lost civilization but the sign and heritage of their ancestors. The enchanting lore of the great Mayan empire implies that they were a lost civilization when in fact, the Maya continue to live to this day. Almost six million Mayans exist today in Mexico, Peru, and other parts of the continent.

For decades following the watershed expedition, researchers used the old-fashioned way of discovering ancient structures, both in the Yucatán Peninsula and in the south. They traversed by foot, kept an eye out for ruins, and if luck was on their side, they would stumble upon a majestic structure. In recent times, this approach has become obsolete with the advent of LIDAR technology. LIDAR, which stands for "Light and Distance Ranging," is a mapping technology that measures and maps different ranges on a terrain. The LIDAR-equipped aircraft fly over the forests and map the land, revealing the hidden secrets beneath. It has helped researchers find the largest Preclassic Mayan ruin located in Tabasco, known as "Aguada Fénix." It is the oldest and largest ceremonial Maya site known to modern man.

Another example is the Maya village of Kiuic, situated in the Yucatán region. The site of Kiuic reveals a large royal palace built atop the remains of a smaller pyramid. Intellectuals think that building on top of a pre-existing structure was a way of legitimizing power. Near the site of Kiuic, archaeologists have found multiple structures, implying that a bigger population traveled to and settled in the region during the Classic Era. The region under discussion has no natural water sources, so the Maya built underground cisterns, called chultuns, for capturing and storing rainwater over long periods. The Maya would form underground chambers and cover them with stucco. Interestingly, the rooftops and plazas of the large pyramid structures were used to capture the rainwater. Made mostly from stone, the magnificent pyramid structures mirror the religious hegemony of the Mayan religion. Some historians associate the pyramids' design – starting with a broad surface and becoming more and more exclusive as it goes up – as a subconscious response to the religious, political, and economic class divide. There is a consensus among archaeologists that the pyramidal structure was a reflection of the sacred caves where the Maya went for worship and other religious purposes. If one looks at the Temple of the Inscriptions in Palenque, the largest pyramid at the site of Palenque – not to be confused with Temple VI of Tikal that is also referred by that name – one finds that its staircase is built beside a nine-chambered platform. The nine chambers represent the nine levels of Xibalba, the Mayan underworld. Nevertheless, it is apparent that the Maya also knew how to adapt the urban design to serve their religious and practical needs.

Researchers denote some Mayan structures as e-groups. An e-group is a stepped pyramid structure built on a west-facing platform. A raised and elongated structure usually exists on the eastern side with a staircase. The staircases were decorated with stucco and exhibit panels of great art. These structures and their parent platform usually stand with the pinpoint precision of astronomical proportions, leading scholars to believe that astronomers used them as observatories. The e-groups gave rise to another prominent architectural group known as the triadic pyramids. Inspired by e-groups, the triadic pyramids would have an elevated platform with a staircase and two structures facing inwards on both sides of the surface. These complexes are mostly oriented towards the west, but in rare cases, they utilize the north-south axis as well. Triadic pyramids are common in the Petén region, especially in Nakbe, where there are more than a dozen of them.

Situated near Kiuic is a prominent city of the ancient Maya: Uxmal. Uxmal is one of the most majestic architectural statements of the Yucatán region. Here, the four extraneous structures of the Nunnery

Quadrangle, with surrounding courtyards and small walls, depict several religious events and entities, including the feathered serpent known as Quetzalcoatl. The structure was constructed as a temple with thirteen doorways in the north building and nine in the south building. The thirteen doorways in the north building represent the levels of the Maya heaven, whereas the nine doorways in the south building mirror the nine levels of the Maya underworld. These four buildings are a perfect representation of the Puuc style of architecture. The Puuc style emanated from the Late Classic era but reached its pinnacle after it, during the Terminal Classic Era. Uxmal also has the House of the Pigeons for ritual and ceremonial purposes and a 24-room House of the Governor that was built in the 10th century.

Another important city of the Yucatán region was Chichen Itza, where archaeologists have found a building believed to be an astronomical observatory. As mentioned before, the Mayans had developed a calendar. In Chichen Itza, one can find an obvious example of how they incorporated their astronomical findings into structural design. An astounding 25-meter pyramid in the city, which the Spanish called "El Castillo," has 365 steps. Another indicator of their mathematical and astronomical prowess is that the shadow falls on the steps of El Castillo on the spring and autumn equinoxes.

The Maya were disciplined in how the city developed its communes over time. They designated different districts to maintain some semblance of the status quo. The Maya integrated their local landscape's topography into their city planning schemes. Some cities were built on top of limestone plains, allowing them to expand towards the horizon, while others were built in the hills, making it easier to construct tall temples and palaces. As cities would grow, the astronomers would decide on an axis based on the region's topography. Then, they would build monumental plazas and palaces according to the predetermined alignment. These religious and governmental structures constituted the heart of the ancient Maya cities. Large causeways connected these monuments across the city.

Alongside the larger structures, they established platforms for hosting secondary structures. Outside the vibrant cultural hubs, there were smaller temples and shrines. However, like any civilization, they had their share of oversights. For instance, experts find no signs of advanced city planning in the Yucatán. There is no apparent grid structure, and cities appear to have expanded haphazardly. This is in stark contrast to other Mesoamerican cities like Teotihuacán that rigidly followed grid plans.

Chapter 4: Mayan Sciences, Religion, and Language

The most fascinating aspect of pre-Columbian New World civilizations is that they evolved right beside the Old World without any contact. Therefore, their alternative timeline presents an interesting challenge to our understanding of how human cultures have progressed over the centuries. Just as there is some resemblance between ancient cultures of the New World and the Old World, there are also vast differences between them. For example, for quite some time, humans have looked back at the invention of the wheel as a landmark achievement in ancient history. Yet, the Maya were completely oblivious to the practical uses of the wheel. They understood the concept, as many artifacts show, but did not put it to good use. Excavated toys and other small devices contain wheels, but no evidence points to the everyday use of wheels. Metal was another inessential tool for the Maya, and they managed to pull off feats of technology and construction without it. Similarly, if one were to invert perspectives, many inventions that were central to the Mesoamerican way of life were absent from Europe, Africa, and Asia.

The Maya used mica for creating a rainbow of glittery paints and developed complex looms for weaving cloth – the former has tons of technological uses today, and the latter is a common item. Research reveals that the Maya were building vulcanized rubber products as well. Comparing the progression of the New World and the Old World might seem like comparing apples and oranges, but the acute observer will find a horde of similarities between the two. The spread and establishment of religious ideas follow parallel trajectories. On both sides of the Pacific, religion has worked as an effective sociological instrument. It has been a productive ideology for bringing communities together and giving a common purpose to the masses. On both sides, superstition and tradition prevailed over logic and reason. Comprehensive languages and scripts were devised to counter this deficiency and to improve effective communication.

How much mathematical and scientific knowledge did the Maya have? How did interpret the world in a religious and spiritual framework? What languages did they speak? Are there any comparisons to be drawn with other cultures?

The Mayan understanding of science and mathematics was closely linked with astronomy since they believed the cosmos had a direct impact on their daily life. The activity of stargazing had such a strong social presence that it found its way into their religion. As mentioned before, the Maya had a strong grasp of the subject, exemplified by the different calendars that were in common use. They could calculate equinoxes and solstices and incorporated this data into their monuments. They also used the astronomical cycles to keep track of planting and harvesting cycles. This remarkable feat is rendered even more impressive when one realizes that they did so without the use of any complex equipment like telescopes. They used to sit in their observatories and stare at the sky.

The Maya used two overlapping calendars in conjunction with each other, collectively known as the "Calendar Round." Many communities across the Guatemalan Highlands used the Calendar

Round and continue to do so. The first calendar, Tzolk'in, translated as "division of days," was a 260-day sacred cycle that dictated religious and ritualistic ceremonies. Today, different tribes use different names for the calendar, including "the sense of the day" and "the organization of time," but nobody knows the ancient name. The second calendar, Haab', was a secular calendar of 365 days, representing the solar year. The Mayan calculations were more precise than the Spanish who arrived in the New World. The Calendar Round completes one iteration after 52 cycles of Haab'.

The tzolk'in calendar developed a significant presence throughout Mesoamerica and can be traced back to the Olmecs and the Zapotecs. Different theories have tried to explain the calendar's origins. One theory draws the reader's attention towards the Mayan numeral system, which has a base of 20, and the Mayan heavens or the upper world, which contains 13 levels. Another theory postulates that the system is closely linked to the middle world or Earth and is in keeping with the period of human gestation. So, the calendar was devised to help midwives keep track of birth cycles. Others maintain that the calendar is highly attuned to the Guatemalan climate and was probably created to track agricultural cycles.

Tzolk'in contains two cycles: the name of the day and a number. There are twenty individual days, and each repetition of the day is numbered from one to thirteen. Each day has an association with events and omens. One day symbolizes death, another is associated with maize and symbolizes abundance, and so on. Tzolk'in was an eminent part of the day-to-day routine of the Maya, and as such, it frequently appears in different codices and inscriptions. They used tzolk'in for various purposes like maize cultivation, setting wedding dates, and associating personality traits according to birthdays.

On the other hand, Haab' consists of eighteen months of twenty days with a final stretch of five days. A date on the calendar consists of the numbered day of the month followed by the name of the month. The last five days of the year, called Wayeb', mark a dangerous and unlucky time for the Maya people. During this time, the portals between the Mayan underworld and the middle world open up, inviting a host of evil spirits and energies. To fight against these misfortunes, the Maya held special rituals and often stay inside and wash their hair until the year is over.

To know the date on the Calendar Round, one needs to know four factors: the day and number in tzolk'in and the numbered day and month in Haab'. The Calendar Round measured time in a loop that would repeat every 52 years. Every date would recur in 52 years, making it impossible to create an absolute chronology of events. To get rid of this issue, a Mayan priest devised another system called the "Long Count" in the 3rd century BCE. The Long Count identified each day against a fixed date in the past. Scholars think the base date is August 11th, 3114 BCE. This date holds tremendous religious value for the Mayan people since it is the presumed date of the Mayan creation. The Long Count groups different sets to tell the date: *baktun* means 144,000 days, *k'atun* means 7,200 days, *tun* means 360 days, *winal* means 20 days, and *kin* means one day. Whenever the Mayans needed to recall an event that did not occur in the same Calendar Round cycle, they would refer to the Long Count. In addition to being inclusive of earlier dates, it was also more legible and concise, making it the format of choice for monuments. The Mayans also used an abbreviated form of Long Count called the "Short Count." The Long Count worked quite similarly to the Calendar Round, but its largest interval, the "Grand Cycle," was much longer – 13 baktuns or 5,139 solar years, to be precise.

The Maya had a penchant for tradition and stories, as epitomized by the religious hierarchy and the disciplined social conduct based on their calendars. While the Maya religion is a belief system, it is, in turn, a part of the larger Maya custom and heritage. These traditions accumulated over multiple centuries, and the belief system accommodated them accordingly. One of these practices is the association of landmarks with religious sentiments. Some communities assigned specific days and dates with certain shrines and mountains, indicating the best time for worshipping there. Most of the rituals would take place near, on, or inside the sacred landmarks. The calendars, cosmology, and geography were used to determine the spiritual importance of each landmark.

The oral transition of rituals from one generation to another depended on the propagation of adventurous tales, which required storytellers. To ensure a fluid flow, a doctrine was established. Individuals could enter the priesthood and other religious orders after rigorous training and evaluation. At the temple of Uxmal, one image of the feathered serpent swallows an individual, and another spits it out. Scholars believe this represents an initiation ritual of the Uxmal Maya where an individual would undergo the most humiliating and meticulous test. The priests would sequester the individual and impose exercises of self-mortification and bloodletting. The corresponding artwork shows individuals piercing their genitals and other body parts. Elsewhere, the Maya usually conducted their priestly initiations inside caves or at other landmarks.

Offerings and other contractual rituals followed strict guidelines, as they were believed to be a connection to the other worlds. The offerings to deities could range from crops like maize, cacao drinks, and honey liquor to pottery, jewelry, animals, and even humans. They also buried sacrificial artifacts and items under floors and altars, but these were not "offerings" in the theological sense of the word. Some Maya buried the bones of their ancestors under their house as a way of showing gratitude and warding off evil spirits. The sacrifices either marked a yearly offering or served as a specific prayer – the Maya often prayed for rain or the end of a drought.

The religious functionaries were tasked with the duties of praying and carrying out sacrifices on behalf of royalty, pure lineages, and the community as a whole. The Maya considered their caves to be the most enlightening and sacred landmarks. The study of these caves reveals some of the earliest Maya art and gives insight into many of their religious habits. Archaeologists have found several signs of shamanism in these caves, implying that the priests made contact with the other world by consuming hallucinogenic substances as part of a cult-like ritual.

Most of what we know about the Maya priesthood today comes from the accounts of Spanish missionaries and the codices that survived the Spanish invasion. Coupled with a large number of inscriptions, these codices have allowed researchers to discern a lot of information about the languages and writing scripts of the ancient Maya. The Maya writing system was a remarkable achievement of pre-Columbian Mesoamerica. There had been several writing systems in Mesoamerica, but none of them were as efficient and complete as the Mayan system. The Olmecs and the Zapotecs were the earliest civilization to develop their scripts, beating the other cultures by a few centuries.

The Mayan writing system was probably preceded by proto-Mayan, a combination of different local languages, including the Olmec language. The earliest examples of the Mayan writing system and its variants date back to the 3rd century BCE. During the Classic period, the Mayan language branched out into two major variants or dialects based on location: the Yucatán Peninsula in the north and Petén Basin in the south. In the 3rd century, the Mayan script started to come into its own and assumed a formal and consistent form. Despite the regional shift, both variants are referred to as the "Classic Maya language" since most Mayan inscriptions, whether in the north or the south, were written in this era and had similarities and overlapping modes and styles.

The Maya script remained in use until the arrival of the Europeans. The Maya used to write on stone monuments, lintels, ceramics, stelae, and most importantly, paper produced from tree bark – the paper was used to assemble codices. Three Mayan codices have been preserved in their original form; others have been partially damaged or lost. These include the Dresden Codex, the Madrid

Codex, and the Paris Codex. A fourth codex, the Grolier Codex, belongs to Toltec-Maya rather than the Maya. Including the inscribed monuments, pottery, and codices, archaeologists have recovered more than 10,000 individual texts to date.

The Mayan writing system has a logosyllabic script composed of individual glyphs connected in succession to form a glyph block. The glyph blocks usually consist of the main signs and corresponding affixes. The main signs can be abstract or material: it can be the image of the described noun or a signal for something a little complex. On the other hand, the affixes hint at the speech elements. The Maya commoners were largely illiterate, and cities and communities had scribes who were responsible for writing during working hours. They charged hefty fees for their services and usually belonged to elite families. Excavations have revealed some writing supplements. In particular, a sculpture in Copán shows scribes with inkpots. Other representations depict women scribes, implying that women participated in art and calligraphy.

The confusing aspect of the term "Maya" is that it does not correspond to any single culture; rather, it combines multiple Mesoamerican cultures with overarching similarities. The northern Maya evolved quite differently from the southern ones, language and all, despite stemming from the same metaphorical well. Ascertaining how much the dialects varied might be a tad too difficult, but as far as written language is concerned, the Maya had a relatively consistent style with subtle variations that stretched all over the region.

PART 2: THE TOLTECS
(674 CE – 1122 CE)

Chapter 5: Chichen Itza and the Toltec Connection

The southern Maya had a different route to regional ascendancy than their northern contemporaries. In the Late Classic Period, Chichen Itza became the primary state of the northern Maya. Located in the east of the Yucatán Peninsula, the site is home to one of the new Seven Wonders of the World: El Castillo. El Castillo is a testament to the Maya's command of cosmology, but the historical significance of El Castillo and Chichen Itza far surpasses their remarkable astronomical proportions. The name Chichen Itza translates to "at the mouth of the well of Itza," Itza being a Maya ethnic group native to Petén Basin in northern Guatemala and some parts of Belize. The Itza probably originated near Lake Petén Itza in Guatemala and formed the Classic Period city of Motul de San José. At the end of the Middle Classic Period and the beginning of the Late Classic Period, they settled at Chichen Itza. However, the word "Itza" could have also simply meant "enchantment of the water" without being a specific reference to the demographic.

The rise of Chichen Itza was not an isolated phenomenon. Chichen Itza turned into a prominent site around the 7th century, but the core site matured during the 8th, 9th, and 10th centuries. This timeline coincides with the fall of two major neighboring cities: Coba to the east and Yaxuna to the south. Chichen Itza might have directly contributed to their downfall – or the unrelated downfall of the cities might have brought more people and more power to Chichen Itza – the exact details are blurry. The Toltecs also rose to power during this time, concluding historians to draw parallels between the growth of both cultures. Some accounts imply a migration from Tula, the Toltec center. At this time, Chichen Itza ascended to a rare stature, exerted influence over the local trade and politics of the region, and led the way in terms of religious ideology. The city could obtain locally unavailable goods by traveling long distances: they acquired gold from Southern America and obsidian from Central Mexico.

Chichen Itza became famous among archaeologists and tourists around the world when John Lloyd Stephens published his book, "Incidents of Travel in Yucatán," in 1843. In 1894, the United States' consul to Yucatán, Edward Herbert Thompson, conducted a detailed examination of the city and took the excavated artifacts back home. In 1926, the Mexican government seized Thompson's plantation, accused him of stealing the artifacts, and proceeded to take control of the ancient site. In 1944, the Mexican Supreme Court decided in favor of Thompson, who was no longer alive. The property was given to his heirs, who sold it to Fernando Barbachano Peon, a tourism pioneer. The land was privately owned until 2010 when the state of Yucatán bought it and handed the reigns of site administration over to Instituto Nacional de Antropología e Historia, Mexico's national institute of anthropology and history.

The remains of Chichen Itza today only hint at the metropolitan's former glory. In its heyday, the city covered at least 5 square kilometers or 1.9 square miles. The population might have risen as high as 50,000, a substantial number for any city in the world at the time. Divided into multiple districts by low walls, it contained around a hundred small pathways that linked sites throughout the city. While the landscape appears flat and concise, archaeologists believe it to be a deception. They think that in a mountainous region like the Yucatán, it would be hard to find such a large and flat piece of land. They are almost certain that the entire area was flattened by the Mayans to develop the city, an act that would have taken quite a long time considering the technology and tools of the time.

Figure 3: Chichen Itza

Let us start with the elephant in the room: El Castillo. Also known as "The Temple of Kukulkan," the giant pyramid is one of the most visited sites on the planet. When the sun sets on the equinoxes, the shadow of a snake writhes down the steps and connects with the sculpted head at the base. Resting on the "Northern Platform," El Castillo was built over a smaller pyramid. The smaller pyramid may not be visible from the outside, but it continues to exist. The structure stands at the height of 30 meters (or 98 feet), while the small temple at the summit is 6 meters (or 20 feet) high. Consisting of nine terraces that recede in size as one moves up, the Temple of Kukulkan is incredibly well proportioned. Studies reveal that El Castillo sits atop a cenote; the city of Chichen Itza has several cenotes – large water bodies used for drinking and sacrificial rites. So far, four cenotes or natural sinkholes have been discovered near Chichen Itza; researchers suspect there may be more. Expeditions have revealed jade, pottery, gold, and human remains at the bottom of some cenotes. The most sacred cenote is located to the north of the core city and was probably used for sacrificial offerings to the rain god Chaac – crops, items of daily use, or human beings. The Maya may have believed that the cenotes were portals to the Maya underworld. So, the location of El Castillo also poses a major question: did the Maya consider the cenote underneath the temple as the most sacred of all? The structure's nine terraces also mirror the nine levels of the underworld. It might just be a coincidence, but that proposition seems rather unlikely.

The Northern Platform also contains the largest Mesoamerican ballcourt. The court has parallel walls with scoring rings at the top. The players would have had to hit a rubber ball through them to win the game. Chichen Itza may have had up to thirteen ballcourts. The sculptures on the courts' parallel walls shine a light on the rules and traditions of the game. The Platform of Eagles and the Jaguars, located adjacent to the ballcourt, depicts Toltec influence. Heading south from the Northern Platform, one ends up at the "Osario Group." It was home to many important buildings of the city like the Osario Temple and the nunnery, Las Monjas. The oldest part of the city is Chichen Viejo.

Various districts of the city have different architectural styles. This either shows the natural progression of the city – the Mayans were not acute city planners – or it shows the prevalence of a heterogeneous, cosmopolitan culture. The blend of migrating factions may have contributed to pluralism in the society. Excavations and subsequent studies regarding the city show increasing signs of Toltec-Maya, rather than just Maya. Consider the Temple of the Warriors, a large complex that is home to a stepped pyramid and a horde of cultural artifacts. A temple in the city of Tula, known as Temple B, is eerily similar to the Temple of the Warriors except in size. Scholars consider the Toltec-Maya connection a unique and unprecedented episode in Mesoamerica.

The architectural similarities between Chichen Itza and the capital city of the Toltecs, Tula, have been a controversial subject over the years. Early scholars noted that Tula has a pyramid that is similar to El Castillo. They theorized that the Toltecs took over Chichen Itza around the 9th and 10th centuries. This helped explain the change in architectural style in the Terminal Classic Era. Some speculated that the original inhabitants of Chichen Itza abandoned the site, and the Toltecs gained control of it. Others believed that the Toltec king, Kukulkan, and his successors invaded Chichen Itza on multiple occasions.

Some of these beliefs have since been refuted, and others are under scrutiny. Today, scholars usually believe that historical accounts from the era imply a migration from Tula to Chichen Itza – the extent of the migration is under debate. One Tula account, in particular, implies that a Tula king traveled towards Chichen Itza. Similarly, an account from Chichen Itza records the arrival of a king from the west. Recent research has shown that most structures of either style were built before the assumed invasion, interference, or arrival of the Toltecs. Radiocarbon dating has revealed that almost all of the structures in question were erected around the same time. The new research also reveals that the Toltec-Maya structures in Chichen Itza are older than the corresponding structures in Tula. Considering this new information, most older theories fail to explain the situation adequately.

Despite these new revelations, scientists lack any real information that will help them understand the introduction of these cultural influences. Modern historians are still working on explaining this phenomenon. Some theorists argue that the trade between the two cities might be the missing link in the story. The people of Chichen Itza were using commodities that can be found in New Mexico and Arizona, leading experts to conclude that they were engaged in long-distance trade. We know that the Maya had established extensive trade routes throughout the region, so they were most likely trading with the Toltecs as well. It is possible that the inhabitants of Chichen Itza, impressed by the Toltec culture, decided to integrate those values into their culture. Another theory postulates that the city's origins hold the key to the mystery. Chichen Itza was a cosmopolitan city in every sense of the word. The destruction of Coba and Yaxuna would have added to the city's population. The prevalence of various cultures would have certainly contributed to the diversity of the style. Moreover, since the prevalent style is Toltec-Maya, Chichen Itza was probably a city of two major ethnicities: the Toltecs and the Maya, leading to a duality of style.

As of yet, there is no definite evidence that shows that the Toltecs controlled Chichen Itza. And, since carbon dating procedures inform us that the structures of Chichen Itza are older than the Toltec structures of the same style, some historians think that we need to invert our perspective. Instead of assuming that the Toltecs influenced the Maya, we must wonder if Chichen Itza influenced Tula. This theory is not widely accepted. Scholars point out that there were Toltec-style buildings in Chichen Itza. Therefore, even if Chichen Itza was the senior city and held sway over the culture of Tula, the Toltec structures in the Mayan city still pose a question mark.

The existence of a connection is not under dispute. While the connection between the two peoples is generally accepted, the lack of information looms large over the historical accounts. As much as theorists have speculated over the nature of their relationship, no concrete knowledge is available. The issue comes down to the lack of evidence; little to no texts survived the Spanish conquest. Scholarly speculations are based entirely on the art and architecture of the cities. Take note that the Maya painted colorful inscriptions and sculptures – a far cry from the monotonous color of the artifacts we see today. Time and climate may have waned the monuments' vibrant look, but archaeologists believe that the Maya were quite fond of colors.

The Mayan city continued to soar until the 13th century, when the neighboring city of Mayapan assumed control. Some Mayan sources explain how this came about. As discussed earlier, the Mayans considered cenotes sacred landmarks. According to the accounts, the ruler of Mayapan jumped into the cenote, made it out alive, and prophesied his rise to power. Research shows that Chichen Itza was looted and plundered at least once. Mayapan may or may not have had something to do with it. By the end of the 11th century, the city was witnessing a decline. Sometime around the 13th century, Mayapan rose to become a major force of the Yucatán. In the 15th century, Mayapan fell into ruins and was abandoned in the 16th century. When the Spanish arrived in the 16th century, they found people residing at Chichen Itza. Whether this population was located in the original city or a settlement close to it remains a matter of some ambiguity.

Chapter 6: The Question about the Toltecs

The Aztecs, comprised of different ethnic groups from all over central Mexico, came to dominate the region in the 14th century. The term "Aztec," like Maya, is an umbrella term – it does not refer to an individual people but to many different tribes and cultures of a similar vein. The Aztec Empire was based on the alliance of three city-states, including the illustrious city of Teotihuacán. Looking at the chronology of the Mayan collapse and the Aztec ascent, one realizes that there is a major gap in the modern understanding of Mesoamerican history. After all, the Classic Maya collapse occurred during the 8th and 9th centuries, and the Aztecs rose to power in the 14th century. The phenomenal gap between these two epochs calls for critical examination. Therefore, the Toltecs are of tremendous interest to modern archaeology.

The Toltecs feature heavily in Aztec texts where their presence conveys a grandiose ideal – a mythical stream of cultural, economic, and political achievement. The Aztecs thought that monarchs were an extension of divine entities, so they claimed that as descendants of the Toltecs - a royal bloodline - they had a divine right to rule. The oral tradition of the Aztecs regales tales of a great people who rose from the ashes of the Classic Maya and commenced a new era in the story of Mesoamerica. The Toltecs probably emanated from eastern and central Mexico and founded the esteemed city of Tula, known in the native Nahuatl language as "Tōllān." In this city, the people lived in buildings made of jade and gold. The Aztecs attributed almost all the artistic and scientific contributions of Mesoamerica to the Toltecs. The origins of Toltecs are shrouded in mystery.

The Aztecs describe the Toltec Empire as a society of warriors that worshipped a storm god – either the Aztec god Tlaloc or the Maya god Chaac. A wise king called Quetzalcoatl ruled the vast kingdom. The Aztec accounts refer to Cē Ācatl Topiltzin Quetzalcoatl as a humble and courageous king who prioritized education amongst the vassals, teaching them to read, write, and measure time. He taught them to work with luxurious metals like gold, jade, and feathers. He trained them in agricultural skills, telling them how to grow cotton and use it to create objects of artistic and practical value. He taught them to raise maize and cacao. The Aztec inscriptions say that Quetzalcoatl was born in 843 and died in 895. You might be noticing minor discrepancies and some exaggeration because we know that maize and cacao were used in Mayan societies long before the 9th century.

The Aztecs further credit Quetzalcoatl with the construction of four prayer houses and a temple for promoting spiritual enlightenment. The temple had majestic columns with meticulous carvings of serpents. After some sorcerers in the city tricked Quetzalcoatl, he fled to the east in shame. When he reached the shore, he burned himself and rose to the sky, metamorphosing into a morning star. In Uxmal, there are clear signs of the cult of Quetzalcoatl. Despite the connection, we are not aware whether an actual individual had anything to do with it or if Quetzalcoatl was a story that reached the area. Most Aztec accounts say that Quetzalcoatl left for the east, but there is a text that serves as an outlier. It says that after burying important artifacts, Quetzalcoatl burned Tollan down to the ground. Our understanding of the feathered serpent god of the

Toltecs and the Aztecs is still quite blurry and offers no clear answers. After all, most of what we know about the Toltecs today has been passed down to us by the Aztecs. Opinions differ on the veracity of different accounts: some call the historical precision of the Aztec accounts into question; others declare them to be semi-mythical accounts.

So, did the Toltec Empire exist, or was it merely a fable told by the Aztecs?

If one were to draw a comparison with other ancient civilizations, one is inclined to notice similarities between the Aztec accounts of the Toltecs and the stories of the Old Testament. Studies have verified the narrative of the sacred Jewish texts to quite an extent. However, historians are still divided on an issue. There is no way to establish the validity of the texts' fantastic elements. Our understanding of ancient texts relies heavily on means that lie beyond the premises of elementary approaches like the Socratic Method. One simply cannot acquire hard-boiled evidence about every little detail, so supposition and intelligent guessing are common techniques in archaeology. Due to the lack of evidence, disagreements are a natural part of scientific and historical discourse regarding Mesoamerican cultures as well. The opinions of modern intellectuals on the Toltec Empire are categorized as historicist perspectives and non-historicist perspectives.

Historicists acknowledge that a large part of the Aztec narrative is mythological, and it would be misleading to take it at face value. However, they think that comparative analysis and critical attention to detail can yield some historical knowledge of genuine value. As such, the Aztec accounts should not be dismissed as unreliable sources. In the late 1850s, a Frenchman, Désiré Charnay, arrived in Yucatán. Inspired by John Lloyd Stephens' books, he started to explore Mesoamerican sites and extensively photographed the architecture, inscriptions, and artifacts. He continued his expeditions for the better part of the mid-to-late 19th century. He raised enough money to follow the journey of Quetzacoatl from Tula towards the Yucatán Peninsula, becoming the first archaeologist to do so. When he arrived at Chichen Itza, a ball court and some serpent columns immediately struck him. Noticing the similarities between Tula and Chichen Itza, he concluded that Tula was the capital city of the Toltecs. His historicist perspective posits that the Toltecs violently took over Chichen Itza. As discussed in the previous chapter, there is no direct evidence that backs up this theory. If anything, recent studies have rendered this perspective quite problematic and rather unsavory.

After the initial excursion, many scholars weighed in on the matter. In the next few years, intellectuals started to see the term "Toltec" in a very different light. They started associating the word "Toltec" with certain cultural traits that appeared in the Guatemalan Highlands, Chichen Itza, and Mayapan during the Postclassic period. These traits are also known as the "Mexican" influences of the Maya. The historicist perspective was the prevalent school of thought for most of the 20th century. Some of these historicist scholars believed that the Toltecs were a distinct ethnic group that either emanated from Tula or settled there eventually. They theorized that the Toltec Empire either dominated or decisively influenced the landscape of central Mexico from the 10th century to the 12th century. According to them, the Aztec myth of Tollan was a reference to the site of Tula. The Aztec term "Tollan" has always been a matter of debate. The Aztecs used it frequently, often referring to the Mexican city-states. Some historians, like Enrique Florescano, posited that it might originally have been a reference to the mighty Teotihuacán, and as time went by, the Mayan texts started to refer to Chichen Itza as Tollan. Other historicists like H.B Nicholson and Nigel Davies were a little skeptical of the prevalent historicist arguments. They felt that they needed to apply critical methods and untangle the mythical elements from the factual accounts.

During the 19th century, Daniel Garrison Brinton – an American historian and ethnologist – argued against the belief that an empire was based on the site of Tula. Subsequent anti-historicists dismiss

Aztec texts and inscriptions as religious texts with minor historical value. Some anti-historicists are completely dismissive of the Aztec stories, arguing that the Toltec Empire is the fourth of the five ages of the Aztecs' religious framework. Most anti-historicists claim that, outside of a few emperors and their battles, any value ascribed to the Aztec tales is a misguided attempt to find answers in places where there are none. They also call attention to the idea that the states of Teotihuacán and Tenochtitlan were the most substantial contributors to the culture of Mesoamerica. Relatively, the Toltec influence falls quite short.

Recent studies have negated historicist views, and comparative analyses of the situation have favored anti-historicist perspectives. The term "comparative analysis" simply refers to the inference of conclusions based on the comparison between two things – documents, processes, objects, or something else. Modern historical research often opts for a comparative approach. In comparative historical research, one examines the relevant historical events by theory building, referencing the current epoch, and comparing the events with other historical events. The approach gains a lot of its momentum by understanding the broader sociological traits and their consequent manifestations. The study of the Toltecs presents the same issues that one usually encounters in comparative historical research. The historical data is incomplete, the scale and complexity of the social systems are unknown, and personal records like memoirs or letters that we have could be and probably are biased.

These days, scholars have started to favor the original approach of Brinton based on a critical evaluation of the accounts. Modern research frames the word "Toltec" quite differently. According to them, the Aztecs reminisced about the sophistication, vigor, and ferocity of Classic and Postclassic Mesoamerican civilizations by granting them a fabled status. Considering that they treated kings as semi-divine figures, this proposition does not appear baseless.

Some modern historians maintain that the task of understanding Toltecs, with our current data, is unsurmountable. The Aztec accounts are incredibly hard to decipher because of their ambiguity. As we know, the Aztecs had a cyclical understanding of time, which further hinders our search for answers. Quetzalcoatl is the biggest example of this misunderstanding because two figures are associated with the name. The first one was the founding father of the Toltecs and a great ruler who exercised his valiance and might on his enemies. The second one was the last ruler of the Toltecs who foresaw the decline of the Toltecs as their power across Mesoamerica withered and whimpered. The Toltec priests forced Quetzalcoatl into a life of shame and humiliation, and he had to leave his homeland. This confusion makes it impossible to differentiate between Quetzalcoatl, the deity, and Topiltzin Cē Ācatl, a historical figure.

The Aztecs were of Nahua ethnicity, and in the Nahuatl language, *Toltec* meant artist, artisan, or wise man. This was in stark contrast to the word, Chichimecayotl, which is a reference to the Chichimecas. Some considered them to be barbarians or uncivilized people who were yet to be urbanized. If we apply this model to the Postclassic and Terminal Classic Periods, the Aztecs could have used the word "Tollan" to refer to any urban center with a respectable reputation and "Toltecs" to refer to its inhabitants. The titles of several places throughout Mesoamerica referenced Tollan. It is also possible that individuals asserted themselves to be Toltecs – descendants of urban nobility – because the Mesoamericans cherished and admired pure bloodlines. This interpretation seems even more plausible when one notices that different settlements of the Itza Mayas, the Aztecs, and the K'iche claim to have been founded by Quetzalcoatl.

In the Postclassic Era, increasing signs of "Mexican" traits started appearing in a large part of Mesoamerica. The usual Toltec traits include the chacmool sculptures found in Tula and Chichen Itza – relief sculptures depicting the feathered serpent – and large galleries with adorned columns. When the Toltec characteristics started to show up in the region, their inclusion into other cultures was selective. The cultures welcomed the Toltec attributes into their way of life - instead of an external force shoving it down their throats. Skeptics do not deny this; however, they ascribe this phenomenon to different events. Teotihuacán may have been destroyed in the Classic Era, but its inhabitants did not suffer the same fate. They lost their homes, were displaced, migrated, and probably took their culture to other parts of the region. The Mexican traits could simply have been the evolution of those cultural ideas in conjunction with the various civilizations of Mesoamerica. In recent years, scholars have refrained from calling Tula the breeding grounds of a great empire. They use the word "Toltecs" to describe the inhabitants of Tula.

These various interpretations serve as different versions of the truth. The objective truth of the Toltecs still eludes us. Some interpretations have fared better than others over time, but that does not speak to their validity. Without any substantial evidence, we cannot claim to know who the Toltecs were, whether the Toltec Empire existed, or what Tula stood for - which brings us to the most intriguing part of the mystery: Tula.

Chapter 7: Tula: City of the Toltecs

Tula is a Mesoamerican archaeological site located in the Mexican state of Hidalgo. Many historians and archaeologists believe it to be the regional center of the Toltec Empire. It exists 75 kilometers north of Mexico City, in the modern city of Tula de Allende. Like Chichen Itza, it is almost a two-hour drive from Mexico City, albeit in a completely different direction. The site lies within alluvial bottoms and houses the Rosas and the Tula rivers. The remains of the ancient city are located on two sides of a low ridge. Tula is a Nahuatl language name that roughly translates to "near the cattails."

The city reached its zenith around 850, and fell into decline around 1150. It was the eminent metropolitan of its era, bridging the gap between the fall of Teotihuacán and the rise of the Aztec center, Tenochtitlan. Like much of the information regarding the Toltecs, modern research provides one with varied interpretations and conflicting viewpoints about the site of Tula.

One must wonder: *When the Aztecs mentioned "Tollan," were they referring to the site of Tula in Hidalgo?*

Figure 4: Tula

Extensive research conducted on the sites and relevant anthropological studies estimate Tula as the likely capital of the Toltecs, and historians have continued to favor this narrative over the years. Before we establish the significance of the site of Tula, we have to demonstrate, as a prerequisite, that Tula was indeed Tollan. Whenever we try to restrict Tollan to any set of archaeological ruins, we tend to encounter a few problems. In the case of Tula, one notices that Tula was considerably large, but it could not possibly have had much influence over the entire region. It participated in trade but did not exert much control beyond its neighboring states. Therefore, it is quite unlikely that it spawned an entire empire of mighty warriors and wise, upstanding civilians. All of this hints at the possibility of semantic overlap. We know that the Aztecs used the word in different contexts, so it is quite possible that Tula was the original Tollan, and afterward, the phrase caught on.

On the other hand, should one venture a little further and arrive at Teotihuacán, one cannot overlook the fact that it had perished centuries before the Toltecs' appearance. Therefore, Teotihuacán seems unlikely to have been the original Tollan. However, some intellectuals postulate that Teotihuacán could have been ravaged and looted by the Toltecs.

If Tollan was a reference to a single, distinct city, it probably referenced the site of Tula, Hidalgo. Furthermore, the site of Tula displays many sculptures depicting the cosmology and mythology of

Quetzalcoatl. The discovery of a glyph that shows the birthday and birth name of the great Toltec leader, Topiltzin Cē Ācatl, further solidifies Tula's position as the center of Toltec activity.

The earliest known settlements at the site of Tula date back to around 400 BCE, with various indigenous tribes inhabiting it over the years. During the Middle and Late Classic Era, the site probably fell under the control of Teotihuacán, as shown by the pottery designs on the site. In the Late Classic Era, the southern Maya lowlands were growing feeble and declining in population. During the 10th, 11th, and 12th centuries, the diaspora of Teotihuacán and the southern Maya was dissolving into the region, leading to new settlements, political alliances, and the development of trade routes. The power vacuum brought more power to the smaller states. During this period, we notice new trade routes and innovative art styles appearing on the sites of Xochicalco, Cholula, Cacaxtla, and, most importantly, Chichen Itza. Observing the Tula ceramics, one finds that they change significantly during this time. Not only that, but the settlements also witnessed their share of dynamism as people started to settle on hilltops. The consequent architecture shows clear signs of pluralism and implies that the new societies were probably multi-ethnic. It is quite feasible that an ethnic group – like the Toltecs – absorbed the dislocated masses and expanded their city.

Tula was established as a small town around 750. If you visit Tula today, you will notice two clusters of structures on the site. One of these is called Tula Chico (small Tula), while the other is called Tula Grande (big Tula). During the Early Classic Period, the city populace was concentrated at Tula Chico. Compared to other sites of the era, Tula Chico has visibly smaller structures. It probably contributed to regional trade and politics in a minor fashion. At the beginning of the Late Classic Period, Tula expanded and turned into an urban populace covering around 1.5 square kilometers. Tula Chico continued to prosper during the Late Classic Era and, at its height, might have spanned five or six square kilometers with a population of

19,000 to 27,000. In the second half of the century, Tula Chico was abandoned, and Tula Grande began to form. Today, some original parts of Tula Chico might be buried under Tula Grande. In the Terminal Classic Era, Tula Grande continued to expand. At its height, the city spanned almost 14 square kilometers and boasted a population of around 60,000. Another 20,000 to 25,000 people populated the city's outer limits.

Like the architects of Teotihuacán, the Toltecs aligned most city structures at 17 degrees east of true north. However, they aligned the first village to the true north. The ceremonial structure of Tula was built on a limestone base that was surrounded in three directions by steep banks. The civic-ceremonial district at the heart of the ancient city is known as the Sacred Precinct. It is a large, quadrangular plaza, surrounded by a couple of L-shaped structures, Pyramid B, Pyramid C, and the Quemado Palace. The city also consists of two Mesoamerican ballcourts and several other large buildings. This entire area hints at many architectural innovations, signifying crucial changes in the city's social life. There is a perceivable expansion of ritual space, and considerable emphasis is placed upon the spiritual guidance of the masses. The Toltecs started to engage in ritual practices in an extravagant, public fashion. With three narrow meeting halls surrounding its three sides, the central plaza can hold up to 100,000 people at a time. The columns of the meeting halls face towards the plaza, and the plaza has almost 1,000 meters of benches embellished with depictions of ceremonies.

The most exotic, fantastic, and appealing structure of the site is, unquestionably, Pyramid B. The pyramid, commonly known as "the Pyramid of Quetzalcoatl" or "the Pyramid of the Morning Star," is a five-stepped pyramid that mirrors the design of the Temple of the Warriors at Chichen Itza. The morning star is a reference to the planet Venus, which holds enormous astrological importance to Mesoamerican civilizations; it disappears at night and reappears in the morning. The evening star symbolizes Quetzalcoatl's time on earth as a human entity, and the Toltecs believed that just like the morning star, he would appear once again. Sometimes, the temple is also referred to as the "Temple of Tlahuizcalpantecuhtli," which roughly translates to the Temple of the Lord of the Dawn.

At the top of the pyramid, one finds four majestic, colossal warrior statues standing at the height of 4.6 meters or 15 feet, called the "Atlantean warriors." Originally, these figures functioned as large columns that supported the temple's roof. The "Atlantean" connotation comes from 19th century North American and European scholars. No feature of the figures implies any kind of Atlantean influence or similarity. Dating procedures approximate that the statues were erected around 750 or shortly afterward.

The Toltecs used basalt stone to build the statues, which is not locally available. Each statue is divided into four sections that are stacked on top of each other. When archaeologists initially discovered them, some sections had fallen to the ground. The statues are probably based on the likeness of four Toltec warriors. The menacing statues tower way above the average human being and instill a spine-tingling aura. Their steadfast eyes convey a stoic calm and a sense of duty towards their fellow brethren. Each figure can be seen wearing a butterfly breastplate and headdresses made of feathers and serpent scales. They carry sun-shaped shields on their backs, spear throwers in one hand, and spears in the other. Their presence at the center of Tula may have been a demonstration of power. These statues reinforce the image of Toltecs as skillful artists and mighty warriors.

The Temple of Quetzalcoatl serves a function of the Tula school of art and architecture. When compared with similar structures in Teotihuacán and Tenochtitlan, the buildings are smaller. This decrease in size mimics another phenomenon: the city of Tula was much smaller in size than the metropolitans mentioned above. The Toltecs may have opted for a reduction in size and scale, but they decorated their structures most affectionately. The five terraces of the main temple portray various natural and supernatural entities like marching felines, birds eating human hearts, and human bodies appearing from the mouth of the feathered serpent. The motif of the feathered serpent eating and expelling humans from the mouth also appears at Uxmal.

The other temple of the city, Temple Mayor or the "Temple of the Sun," is no longer intact, but it used to serve as the city's main temple. In its original form, it would have been the larger of the two main temples. Beside the main temple and across a narrow alley, one looks upon the burnt remains of the Palace Quemado, the probable residence of the Tula ruler. In front of the Palace, one stumbles upon a few headless chacmools – reclining sculptures. Out of the seven chacmools, just one has survived in its complete form. The friezes in the area illustrate the story of Mixcoatl and Tlahuizcalpantecuhtli via colorful depictions of eagles, jaguars, coyotes, birdmen, and other creatures. Mixcoatl is presumed to be the father of Quetzalcoatl, whereas Tlahuizcalpantecuhtli is the form of the feathered serpent upon his inevitable return.

The most impressive artistic statement, Coatepantli, or the Wall of Snakes, sits opposite to these friezes. The best-known artwork at Tula was made from local sedimentary stone and contains brightly colored reliefs. It shows serpents devouring human beings, per the motif of Quetzalcoat's worship and human sacrifice rituals. Another important artwork is the frieze of the Caciques that lies in a hall connecting the main pyramid with the main plaza. Art historians interpret the nineteen men shown in it as either local chiefs or merchants. Modern Tula has an on-site museum and an orientation center that displays stone sculptures and other archaeological discoveries. In general, the subjects of the Toltec art are quite similar to that of Teotihuacán and reinforce the same religious believes and ideologies.

Most Mesoamerican experts believe that the establishment of inter-regional trade routes brought a lot of traffic from Teotihuacán. Trade networks were engaged in the exchange of obsidian and salt by the 4th century. The steady flow of traffic increased exponentially after the fall of the Teotihuacán. In the 8th century, the markets of Tula started to reach their maximum potential. Aristocrats, artisans, and rich merchants were elite figures in the central city, whereas farmers lived in the city's outer vicinity. Researchers have proposed that the area received more rainfall during the Classic Era, accounting for the lack of natural irrigation. Excavations have revealed proof of the cultivation of chili peppers, corn, beans, squash, amaranth, and maguey. Like the Maya and many other Mesoamerican civilizations, corn was the major source of food. At the time, Tula was very rich in obsidian, and, thus, it was part of an important trade route. The city had an agricultural base, but many people were involved in mining and crafting obsidian.

Tula witnessed a sudden demise during the 11th and 12th centuries when a significant portion of the population abandoned their houses and migrated to other areas. Not much is known about the collapse of the Toltecs. According to some, natural disasters made it impossible to sustain life in the region; others theorize that internal strife ruined the city. The internal strife theory ties in with the story of Quetzalcoatl, who was betrayed by local chiefs. Despite the fall, Tula continued to exist until the Spanish invasion of the Americas.

Tula has been overlooked compared to other great cities of Mesoamerica like Teotihuacán, Monte Alban, and Tenochtitlan. It has not been the target of extensive research like the other cities. Nevertheless, the lack of research constitutes a fraction of the issues one faces when confronted with the puzzle of Tula. The overwhelming lack of evidence makes it difficult to make a consistent hypothesis. Whatever theory you might lean toward, the fact remains that the Toltecs' impact on the region cannot be underestimated. Some have proposed that it was a small site with relatively little effect on the broader landscape of Mesoamerica. Recent excavations have revealed large residential complexes just outside the ceremonial center, subsequently negating the "uninfluential" premise. The impact of Toltec art spread throughout the land. When the Spanish arrived in the New World, Quetzalcoatl was already a cult figure, widely worshipped all over Central America. It had even seeped its way into Aztec ideology.

Chapter 8: Cē Ācatl Topiltzin: The Mythic Toltec King

In 1504, Hernan Cortes, a Spanish teenager, arrived in the New World. After aiding Diego Velázquez in the conquest of Cuba, he was elevated to a higher designation and was due for inland Mexico. However, his superiors changed their minds and ordered him to stay. In 1519, the Spanish conquistador ignored his superior's orders and headed inland to secure Mexico for colonization in an act of mutiny. After stopping briefly in Trinidad to stock up on resources and hire extra help, he reached the Yucatán Peninsula. In the name of the Spanish crown, he defeated foe after foe. Throughout his journey, he took full advantage of the tribal dispositions of the indigenous people. By turning one tribe against the other, he would side with some tribes and vanquish others. When the Spanish reached the Aztec capital of Tenochtitlan, they had a massive army. The Aztec king, Montezuma, allowed Cortes and his army to enter the city to learn about their weaknesses. He awarded gifts of gold, jade, and obsidian to the Spanish army. In a letter to King Charles, Cortes claims that the Aztecs believed him to be Quetzalcoatl or an embassy of Quetzalcoatl. The belief of Quetzalcoatl was so widespread throughout the Mesoamerican land that it even rendered kings vulnerable to invaders.

Hernan Cortes took Montezuma captive and sacked the grand city of Tenochtitlan, essentially bringing an end to Aztec glory. The Aztecs associated Montezuma's hesitation towards conflict with his belief in the return of the feathered deity. Nevertheless, one must realize that this story came out after the Spanish had taken over the city, which makes many historians wonder if the Aztecs fabricated the story to save face. While Montezuma was providing treats to the Spaniards, his army had started a war with the Spanish army outside the city. Montezuma may have simply treated the Spanish as potential allies who could have helped him enlarge his kingdom. Whether the tale of the Aztec king's belief in Quetzalcoatl is true or not, it serves as a delightful distraction to rationalize defeat. The distraction worked only because of the prevalent faith in the feathered serpent of Tollan. In modern literature, some scholars take issue with the phrase "the cult of Quetzalcoatl" because it was much less a cult than a reverent religious and political ideology that engulfed the entire region.

Was Quetzalcoatl a single individual - a Toltec emperor of profound insight and raw, potent vigor? Alternatively, was he an idea that extended beyond an individual figure and encompassed something broader?

Quetzalcoatl translates literally to "serpent of precious feathers" and loosely to "Quetzal-feathered serpent." A quetzal - to be precise, a resplendent quetzal - is a bird that can be found in different parts of Mexico. The Guatemalan flag has an image of the bird, and it happens to be the national bird of the nation as well. Quetzalcoatl belonged in the most esteemed company of Aztec gods, along with Tlaloc, Huitzilopochtli, and Tezcatlipoca. Most people believed him to be the god of sun, wind, and learning, among other things. Different interpretations of Quetzalcoatl existed in different regions, and it would be naïve to look for consistencies among these different narratives. In certain eras, some regions thought of him as the god of vegetation while others associated him with the planet Venus, arts, craft, and knowledge. For instance, the Huastec people of central Mexico associated him with Ehécatl, the wind god, whose attire was quite like their own. The Temple of Quetzalcoatl, located in the Aztec city of Tenochtitlan, is a circular structure because it is believed that the round shape of the architecture was symbolic of wind. Sharp edges are obstacles to the wind, whereas circular shapes seem to aid its dynamism. Similarly, in the states of Veracruz and San Luis Potosi in east-central Mexico – which were home to the Huastec people – one registers the same observation.

Detailed drawings of Quetzalcoatl show him adorned with quetzal feathers and wearing an ornate talisman around his neck. Such stones and jewelry represented different elemental forces of the cosmos. The earliest known act of the feathered serpent's worship dates to around the first century BCE or the first century CE, whereas the earliest iconographic depiction of the deity dates back to around 900 BCE on an Olmec site. In the Olmec depiction, a serpent ascends behind a person engaged in a ritual. This artwork may prove that a divine feathered serpent existed in the Mesoamerican religious pantheon for quite some time; however, historians emphasize that the specific deity of Quetzalcoatl appeared in the Classic Era. There are also a few representations of feathered serpents in Teotihuacán during the Preclassic Era, but in these images, the feathered serpent was drawn as a primal entity with no human features. The human features started to appear during the Classic Era. After the fall of Teotihuacán, the cult of the feathered serpent started to gain prominence. Historians attribute this to the iconography and inscriptions found at different sites across central Mexico like Cholula and Cacaxtla. In particular, Cholula might have been the most prominent center of Quetzalcoatl worship over the following years.

Quetzalcoatl is often conflated with the Toltec king, Cē Ācatl Topiltzin, who ruled a sophisticated and vicious empire during the 10th century. The title, Cē Ācatl Topiltzin Quetzalcoatl, roughly translates to "Our Prince One-Reed Precious Serpent." Several tales recall the life and genius of the Toltec emperor. He was born in Tepoztlan on "1 Acatl," which corresponds to May 13, 895. Accounts differ when it comes to his parents.

There are many different tales of how Quetzalcoatl came to be. According to one story, he was born to the Aztec deity Chimalman, meaning "shield-hand," who was a virgin. According to another story, she swallowed an emerald and conceived Quetzalcoatl. The most popular belief is that his father was Mixcoatl, another Toltec deity and presumably an earlier Toltec king. The story goes that Mixcoatl shot an arrow at Chimalman, who got pregnant and gave birth nine months later. Mixcoatl, which means "Cloud Serpent," was the god of war, fire, and hunting. In drawings and sculptures, he can be seen wearing red-striped clothing and a black mask over his eyes. The god of the morning star, Tlahuizcalpantecuhtli, who is the second rendition of Quetzalcoatl - as the morning star -, also has the same features. Moreover, Mixcoatl carries hunting gear, a bow, and arrows, the likes of which can be seen on the Atlantean statues at Tula. The Aztecs revered Mixcoatl but not as much as they revered some of their other deities. Many indigenous groups like the Otomi and the Chichimecs highly appreciated Mixcoatl. At the ancient sites of Tlaxcala and Huejotzingo, people worshipped him as the central deity.

In his early childhood, Topiltzin proved his mettle as a fierce warrior. Tales credit him for leading his people to the city of Tollan, where he served as a Toltec priest. Most Mesoamerican cultures, including the Maya, Toltecs, and Aztecs, emphasized tribal conflict, war, and human sacrifice. Both themes feature heavily throughout Mesoamerican history. Even some European invaders noted that the indigenous people belonged to a strict tribal culture and were often at war with each other over simple disputes. After all, the invaders exploited this weakness to a great extent, working on the policy of divide and conquer. All this serves to illuminate the statue of Topiltzin among the Mesoamerican civilizations and his humanist reputation among his vassals. The Toltecs saw him as the single most eminent leader in terms of spiritual and sociological resolve. His preference for peace and restrain led him to preach sophisticated and cultured ideals and abolish all human sacrifice. Myths describe that Quetzalcoatl avoided offering humans as sacrificial offerings. Instead, he opted for birds, snakes, butterflies, and other animals. He also swore priests to celibacy and refrained them from using intoxicating substances. We know that the Maya had ritualistic ceremonies in underground caves where they used hallucinogenic substances.

According to the tales, Topiltzin traveled across the land, conquering some settlements and preaching his values to others. He even established new societies and communities using his spiritual faculties. At this point, accounts differ as to what happened with Topiltzin. Some believe that after spreading his word across the land, he set off to the east, convinced that he would find his holy resting place there. Others believe he traveled to Tlapallan, a region on the Gulf Coast of Mexico, where he used a pyre to offer the ultimate sacrifice. By burning and shedding his skin, he was transformed into the Morning Star. Another version states that he embarked on a raft of snakes and disappeared over the horizon to the east.

After Tollan, Cholula is the most important city in regard to Quetzalcoatl. In its heyday, Cholula was the second most populated city in all of Mexico, with a population of around 100,000. The city's population started to decrease in the 8th century, but it remained a hub of religious activities for the next few centuries. Today, Cholula is a tourist attraction for its Great Pyramid, the largest archaeological site of a pyramid in the New World. It is the largest monument ever constructed anywhere throughout history and was built in honor of the feathered serpent. Mythology dictates that after escaping a flood, a giant named Xelhua built the pyramid. In truth, it was probably built in four exhausting stages from the 3rd century BCE to the 9th century CE. By the time construction had finished, the pyramid was six times the size of its original proportions. A Mesoamerican school of thought believed that Topiltzin would return to reclaim Cholula.

Chronology has been a persistent issue with Quetzalcoatl. Cholula's apex was already behind it in the 8th century, and Topiltzin came to power in the 10th century. There is a massive gap between the two events. Since Mesoamerican cultures thought of their kings as semi-divine figures and their understanding of time was cyclical, Topiltzin possibly built upon the conquests of his predecessors. According to Fernando de Alva Cortés Ixtlilxóchitl, a historian of partial Aztec descent, Topiltzin ruled during the 10th century. According to another document, Codex Ramirez, Topiltzin ruled during the 12th century.

The Aztec rulers used religious leverage to gain power, empowering the myth of the Toltec emperor whenever it suited them. As heirs of the Quetzalcoatl bloodline - real or claimed - they asserted that they were the rightful successors to the throne. The diffusion of religious sentiment allowed them to earn the throne and keep it. They could always fall back on the running excuse that they were merely keeping it warm for the feathered serpent. Concocting a religious ideology allowed them to tap into the collective subconscious of the vassals. They were able to convince people of ideas and rituals that were in complete contradiction to Topiltzin's teachings. For instance, they began performing large ceremonial human sacrifices that had been abolished in the Toltec's prime epoch. The Aztecs continued this cycle of lies and deception well into the Postclassic and Colonial times.

Excluding minor and circumstantial evidence, all these tales have been relayed to us via five major sources. The first source, *Historia de los Mexicanos por sus pinturas,* was written by an unknown Spaniard in an attempt to capture the story of the Toltecs. This version is quite brief and possibly inaccurate, probably due to a lack of understanding of the indigenous languages. According to this version, the unnamed mother dies after giving birth to Topiltzin. As he grows up, Topiltzin spends seven years in the quiet sanctity of mountains. At this time, he performs bloodletting rituals and prays with resolve. The gods bestow his wish to become a great warrior, and he starts to wage war and becomes popular among the masses, elevating him to the position of emperor. For 42 years, he maintains peace and harmony in his kingdom but is asked to leave the city of Tollan at the end. He passes through towns, establishes villages, and arrives at Tlapallan only to die the very next day.

In a translation by Catholic friars, called the "Libro de oro y tesoro indico," Topiltzin is recorded as the son of a leader of Teotihuacán. He erects a monument in the memory of his murdered father, takes revenge on his killer, and sets off for Tollan. A translation by Frenchman André Thevet places him as the son of Mixcoatl and Chimalman. The mother dies at birth, and the father is killed by Topiltzin's brothers. He avenges his father's killers and migrates to the city of Tollan. In this version, he serves as an emperor for 160 years. In the end, he flees to Tlapallan once again. A fourth translation was written by a native, the "Leyenda de los soles," or the "Legend of the Suns," which elaborates on the parents of Quetzalcoatl. The fifth source, known as "Florentine Codex," is a collection of texts gathered from native informants.

In all these versions, the Aztec god, Tezcatlipoca, translated as "smoking mirror," is responsible for ousting Topiltzin from Tollan. After Quetzalcoatl struck Tezcatlipoca down and transformed him into a jaguar, he retaliated by striking down Quetzalcoatl. He is often described as the arch-nemesis of the serpent god Quetzalcoatl.

Chapter 9: Tula's Collapse and the Toltec Diaspora

What goes up must come down.

The statement has been valid since before an apple landed on Isaac Newton's head. Its scientific implications may be relatively modern, but in the subject of history, plenty of precedents could serve as our guiding principle. We can see the idea repeatedly manifested throughout history. Mesopotamia was home to the glory and might of impenetrable empires, but all of them had to fall. When the time came, even the Western Roman Empire, the greatest superpower of its era, could not escape the clutches of inevitable demise. With the fall of Constantinople, the Eastern Roman Empire fell as well. The fall of the Western Roman Empire and the Eastern Roman Empire are separated by almost ten centuries. For some empires, it takes centuries to crumble, each conquest a mere tally in the larger scheme of things. For others, the fall is often quick and callous. It comes like a bolt of lightning, felling everything in its path like dominoes. Even in individuals and stories, in arts and literature, the rule holds immeasurable value. The most fascinating aspect of Adam's story is the fall. In music, a crescendo means nothing without the rumbles that precede it.

In the case of the Toltecs, the fall was quick and unforgiving. It all started with the death of Cē Ācatl Topiltzin or Quetzalcoatl. Understanding the fall of Toltecs requires a brief detour. To appreciate the depth of events, it is important to gain an understanding of the Toltecs' rise to power.

Codex Chimalpopoca, an Aztec manuscript, reveals the stories of Quetzalcoatl in three stages. According to the first part of the codex, Anales de Cuauhtitlan – meaning the "Annals of Cuauhtitlan" – during their initial migrations, the Toltecs reached Manenhi. They renamed this land to Tollan and established a theocratic system, which they quickly abandoned in favor of a monarchy. Some migrants settled in the city, whereas others traversed further west in search of new territories and villages. The scholarly disputes regarding chronology are prevalent in this document as well. Different people interpret the dates of the document differently. Some think that the date of the Toltecs' arrival in Tollan belongs to the 7th century, while others translate it to the 8th century. The second part of the codex deals with deities and religion, and the third part contains the Leyenda de los soles. According to some sources, when they arrived at Tollan, the leader of the Toltecs was a man name Huemac. Some intellectuals believe that the Toltecs migrated from the deserts in the northwest, arrived at Culhuacan first, and then proceeded to Tollan. Others say it was Chalchiutlanetzin, and some maintain that it was Cē Ācatl Topiltzin Quetzalcoatl. Some researchers think that Quetzalcoatl was merely a rank the Toltecs associated with not just Topiltzin, but all of their leaders.

The Toltec demographic belonged to different tribes, including Nonoalcas and Chichimecas. According to the Florentine Codex, the Nonoalcas were an important ethnic group at Tollan. On the other hand, Chichimecas were the "inhabitants of Chichiman," and Chichiman means an "area of milk." They were part of a nomadic tribe that was usually on the move. During the Late Classic and Postclassic Era, they wore minimal clothing that only obscured their genitalia, used and ate berries, roots, and hunted animals. This was a function of their minimal lifestyle. They could not afford luxuries, nor did they have time for innovation, so instead of wearing clothes that covered them completely, they preferred to paint their bodies. Because of their pluralist roots, the Toltecs were able to establish contact and trade with other tribes.

Hidalgo is bordered by San Luis Potosi in the north, Puebla in the east, Tlaxcala in the southeast, Queretaro in the west, and Veracruz in the northeast. As the Toltec influence started to grow in the region, it reached La Huasteca in the north. La Huasteca includes parts of Veracruz, Hidalgo, Queretaro, Puebla, San Luis Potosi, and other modern states. Here they encountered two major tribes: the Otomi people and the Huastec people. The existence of people in this region dates to the 10th century BCE, making them one of the earliest civilizations of Mesoamerica. The Otomi tribe were probably the original inhabitants of the site, predating the Nahuatl speakers by several centuries. The Otomi were nomads as well and even contributed to the population of Teotihuacán. All this information ties into the fall of the Toltecs.

According to some fables, Tezcatlipoca appeared before the king, Quetzalcoatl, in the form of an older man and offered him an elixir that would make him younger. This was a deceitful offering as the drink was nothing more than an alcoholic beverage. Topiltzin called for his sister, the princess, and they both indulged in the hazy delights of alcohol. In their drunken stupor, they engaged in scandalous behavior, which left Topiltzin shamed and embarrassed to the core. You might remember that in another tale, the priests were responsible for betraying Topiltzin, but here it is Tezcatlipoca in the form of an older man. Parallels exist between the two narratives as most priests in the city could very well have been old males.

Disgraced and humiliated, Quetzalcoatl left Tollan and headed for Tlillan-Tlapallan. The death or exile of Quetzalcoatl left a hole in the once-prosperous region. The event sowed the seed of discontent and internal strife in the community, which brought about intense political and civil instability. Civil war broke out in Tollan between the supporters of Tezcatlipoca and the supporters of Quetzalcoatl. Most Nonoalca people were adherents of Quetzalcoatl and preferred his humanist ideals, including his contempt for human sacrifices. On the other hand, the followers of Tezcatlipoca's ideology, mostly descendants of the Chichimeca tribe, believed in the supreme power of mass processions and public sacrifices. This can also be seen in the design and architecture at Tula, where the ceremonial structures get larger as the people switch from Tula Chico to the new district.

Around 1000, Tula started to witness agricultural issues. The climate began to dry up, and a shortage of rainfall followed. The agricultural sector did not produce enough corn, their staple crop, to feed the whole city, and with more problems rearing their heads, it failed to reach its minimum target. With the famine, the internal ethnical discord between the Nonoalca and the Chichimeca intensified. Eventually, Tezcatlipoca's worshippers proved too much for the cult of Quetzalcoatl. The devotees of the feathered serpent finally tasted defeat at the hands of their adversaries.

Some authors mention that after the death of Topiltzin, the Toltecs started to migrate from Tollan to other cities at an unprecedented pace. The civil war in Tollan and the consequent defeat probably prompted this migration. Most of them left for the Yucatán Peninsula, where they finally ended up at Uxmal. The most powerful site in western Yucatán, Uxmal, was taken over by Toltec invaders around 1000. After 1100, construction in the city slowed down dramatically, and by 1200, it seems to have ceased altogether. Quetzalcoatl was probably introduced in the Itza region in the late 10th century. The Itza were descendants of the Putun Maya, famous for their Puuc architectural style, and the Toltec Maya. It is probable that the Itzans, of partly Toltec descent, welcomed the Toltec migrants to the Yucatán Peninsula. Around this time, the introduction of Mexican traits increased significantly in the Yucatán region. It is important to notice that the pyramids at Chichen Itza predate similar structures in Tula, so the migrations could have been taking place for some time.

When things took a turn for the worse, even the local Chichimeca started leaving the city, which encouraged even more civil disorder. The natural disasters – climate change and soil leeching – added fire to the fuel. Around 1150, a lot of Tula inhabitants had abandoned their living quarters. Just like in Teotihuacán, most structures were burned and destroyed. The ceremonial center in the heart of the city was burned during the 12th century.

Many exiled groups ended up going to the modern state of Puebla, specifically the city of Cholula. Cholula dates to the 2nd century BCE and was an important trading post for the region during the Postclassic Era. Around Tula, there were no natural water bodies to help the city with irrigation or to fulfill the public's drinking needs. This was not the case in Cholula, where rainfalls were abundant in the summer, and the city was surrounded by snowy mountains. In the summer, the snow from the mountains melted and flowed down. These favorable conditions might have beguiled the famine-ridden exiles. Furthermore, the city was no stranger to an influx of foreigners. During the Late Classic Era and the Early Postclassic Era, the Olmec-Xicallanca, a group from the Gulf Coast, had taken over the city and made it their capital. Around 1200, the Toltecs – most of them from the Chichimeca background – took over the city.

Briefly, after the Spanish conquest of the Aztecs, a Dominican friar by the name of Diego Durán wrote a few seminal texts about the Aztec culture. In his work, "The History of the Indies of New Spain," also known as the "Duran Codex," he weaves together the story of the Aztec creation as well as the history of the region leading up to the Spanish conquest. Duran writes that around 1115, the northern tribes, including but not restricted to Chichimecas, Otomi, and Huastecs, started to launch attacks against different domains of Tollan. After some vicious and violent battles, the Toltecs were on the back foot. Both sides were taking heavy losses. War makes people appeal to their gods, and so, human sacrifice prevailed as the common form of prayer. According to Duran, Huemac, who is referred to in some texts as the first ruler of Tollan, left the city with his proletariat and migrated to the city of Xaltocan, an Otomi city. Huemac had lost the trust of the people. They split up into different groups, abandoned him, and went their separate ways. In 1122, Huemac, faced with degradation and humiliation, hanged himself in the city of Chapultepec. The people of Teotihuacán controlled Chapultepec during the Classic Era. The Toltecs referred to Chapultepec, Hidalgo as the "Grasshopper Hill." Archeologists have found remains of a Toltec altar on the hill's summit.

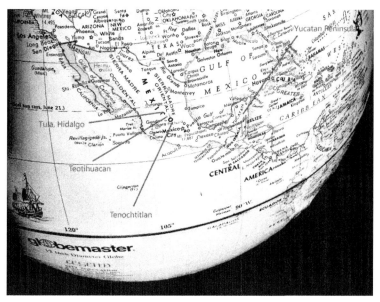

Figure 5: Geography of Mesoamerica

Tollan had been abandoned, and the Toltecs had spread not just in the Valley of Mexico – but all across Mesoamerica. A small population still existed at the ruins of Tollan. Tula fell under the reign of a nearby city-state called Culhuacan, which served as a haven for the aristocrats of the Toltec capital. Culhuacan was under the control of Teotihuacán for most of the Middle Classic Period. Traditional stories dictate that it was the first Toltec city and was founded by Mixcoatl, the father of Quetzalcoatl, probably sometime around the

8th century. Culhuacan, which survived until the 14th century, was a predominantly Toltec city with Chichimeca influence.

City-states like Culhuacan were known as "altepetl," which translates to "the water, the mountain," in Nahuatl. The Toltecs diffused into the region, and several city-states – or altepetl – took over the dominions formerly ruled by the Toltecs. Most Toltecs started using the term *Quetzalcoatl,* willy-nilly to align themselves with the royal bloodline. This enabled them to land high designations in different cities across the region. This overuse of the term *Quetzalcoatl* is one of the main reasons researchers find it so hard to distinguish between different rulers of the Toltecs.

The Toltecs had finally dispersed into various fractions. The fall of the Toltecs brought about a power vacuum in Mesoamerica. The incessant conflict was a pragmatic reality in pre-Columbian Mesoamerica, and during this time, different tribes started egregiously going against one another in a bid to come out on top. From the ashes of the Toltecs rose a culture that would go on to become the hallmark of Mesoamerican civilization, the Aztecs. With Toltec heritage now the standard of nobility across Mesoamerica, it is not surprising that the Aztecs hitched their wagon to the idea of being Toltecs' descendants.

Chapter 10: The Rise of the Aztecs

The Aztec Empire was the biggest empire of Mesoamerica. At its apex, it controlled most of northern Mesoamerica and imposed its will and ideals on neighboring states. When the word "Aztec" is used, modern terminology tends to treat it as a reference to the alliance of three Nahuatl-speaking city-states in central Mexico. In broader terms, they were Nahua people who developed city-states in central Mexico after arriving from the north. Their rise was certainly not an isolated phenomenon and came about as a result of Toltec dispersion. Just like the Toltecs benefited from the Classic Maya Collapse of the 8th and 9th centuries, the Aztecs gained from the collapse of a concentrated Toltec rule.

We know the Aztecs rose to prominence in the Postclassic Period of Mesoamerican chronology. But where did they come from?

As we have witnessed with the Maya and the Toltecs, the accounts of the Aztecs are largely supernatural and mythical. They contain supernatural beings, individuals, sites, and phenomena that physically manifest themselves on Earth. Ethnohistorians have extracted tons of information from studying these tales and other pieces of archaeological evidence. The lineage of the Nahuatl-speaking people, or the Nahua, goes back to the Chichimec people. As discussed before, Chichimec were nomadic people who migrated from the north to the Valley of Mexico. In the north, they used to reside in San Luis Potosi, Zacatecas, and Guanajuato. San Luis Potosi was home to Otomi and Chichimec people. Zacatecas, roughly translated from Nahuatl as "where there is abundant grass," was the home of different ethnic groups that were often at war with each other. Guanajuato had inhabitants since the 8th century BCE approximately. Their influence continued to spread throughout the region and reached Zacatecas, Hidalgo, Queretaro, and other regions. They are often associated with the Toltecs because the decline of their cities happened alongside the decline of the Toltecs.

The Nahua legends speak of seven tribes that lived in the place of seven caves. Each cave was associated with a Nahua tribe: Xochimilca, Tlahuica, Acolhua, Tlaxcalteca, Tepaneca, Chalca, or Mexica. For most of these tribes, the story of migration is quite similar. They claim their place of origin to be Aztlan, "the Place of Herons." The word Aztec derives from the word "Aztlan" and translates to the "people from Aztlan." Whether Aztlan is a mythical place or a historical one is a matter of debate. Those who believe it to be real place it somewhere in northwestern Mexico or the southwest US. Diego Duran details a series of events in which the Aztec emperor, Montezuma I, sent an expedition to find the true location of Aztlan. At the time, the continent was not aptly mapped, making it hard to pinpoint a precise location. In the latter half of the 20th century, Mexican scholars started to speculate that an island called the Mexcaltitán de Uribe may have been the original birthing place of the Aztecs. Nobody knows if there is some truth to this proposition, but the site has recently started gaining tourists' attention.

According to the records, a drought took over the lands of northern Mexico and the southwestern US, forcing the Chichimeca tribes to migrate and arrive in central Mexico. After the earlier tribes arrived in the valley, they started to settle down and create small city-states or altepetl. The ruler of each state, called the Tlatoani, received tribute from all over the land and oversaw trade, religion, litigation, and military. In the beginning, the city-states kept meddling in each other's affairs and igniting needless disputes. With the incessant routine of conflict, none of the states gained much ground.

After two centuries of migrations, Mexica, the last tribe to arrive after the fall of the Toltecs, reached the Valley of Mexico. In the Aztec codices, the Mexica people can be seen carrying idols of their patron deity, Huitzilopochtli. Legend has it that the Mexica were eager to find a sign relayed to them by the Huitzilopochtli. In particular, they were looking for "an eagle with a snake in its beak, perched on a prickly pear cactus."

Around 1250, the Mexica reached the Valley but could not find any good agricultural land. They became vassals of Culhuacan, the city-state of choice for the displaced aristocrats of Tollan. The city gave them Chapultepec, the place the Toltecs called the grasshopper hill. Chapultepec was relatively infertile, so Mexica could not farm there. In the end, the Mexica ended up serving as mercenaries for the state of Culhuacan. At one point, Culhuacan called upon the services of Mexica on the battlefield, and they obliged. As a reward, the grateful emperor sent one of his daughters to govern over the Mexica. On the orders of one of their gods, the tribe killed the daughter by skinning her alive. In a fit of fury, the emperor initiated an offensive against the Mexica. The Mexica were driven from the land.

The nomads roamed free until they reached Lake Texcoco, where they saw the sign of Huitzilopochtli. The piece of land was right in the middle of a marsh, and there was no solid ground to stand. They established a settlement there in 1325 and named it Tenochtitlan. The city's unhospitable location served as a blessing in disguise. There was no easy access to the city; it was only reachable by boats. The city was defensibly sound, and the unusual landscape was great for fending off attackers. Thanks to the impenetrable defense, trade witnessed a boom, and the city started to grow exponentially. The Mexica started to build residential complexes. Aqueducts were set up to provide fresh water to the city. In the heart of the city, they designed a sacred precinct where they built Mesoamerican ballcourts, schools, and quarters for the priests. The Mexica had been awestruck by the magnificence and grandeur of Teotihuacán and Tula. They aspired to reach the level of sophistication and prestige of the great Toltec cities. They believed Teotihuacán was a sacred and holy site and carried ornaments and objects from the city to use in Tenochtitlan. They started erecting palaces and constructed the breathtaking Templo Mayor, also known as Huey Teocalli. The great temple was devoted to Huitzilopochtli and Ehecatl.

Huitzilopochtli was the ultimate god of war, and the Aztecs offered him sacrifices to attain his blessing on the battlefield. The origin mythologies talk about Huitzilopochtli as the youngest of four sons. One of his brothers was Quetzalcoatl. Their parents, two gods, had created the universe. They instructed them to bring peace, harmony, and order to the world. So, they created the male and female forms, and the Earth and the Sun. Initially, Huitzilopochtli may not have been the chief deity of the Mexica and may have been elevated to the stature of Quetzalcoatl, Tezcatlipoca, and other gods after the Aztecs found his sign in the valley.

The Mexica had shown their valor and fortitude time and time again. They quickly developed a reputation as mighty warriors. This was especially important in the Postclassic Era because all the tribes were consumed in the habitual back-and-forth. When the Mexica rose as a force to be dreaded and feared, they quickly gained the respect of neighboring tribes. The Mexica had allied with the state of Azcopotzalco – the capital city of the Tepanec people ruled by the emperor Tezozomoc – and paid tribute to them. The Tepanecs spoke the Nahuatl language and shared the same religious pantheon as the Aztecs. The Mexica aided the growth of Azcopotzalco, and it started to expand as a tributary empire. The only real problem Mexica faced at the time was a lack of legitimacy. The emperor of

Mexica was not considered a real king. To alleviate this, they sent a proposal to a ruler of Culhuacan, asking for the hand of his daughter. The request was granted. In 1372, the son from the wedding, Acamapichtli, became the first emperor, or tlatoani, of Tenochtitlan.

Texcoco, the city of the Acolhua people, was growing in the east of the basin. It had originally been founded by the Chichimecs, but the Acolhua people purged them from the city and took over. Tensions were running high between the Acolhua and the Tepanecs. Matters escalated, and war broke out between the two. The Mexica sided with their allies, the Tepanecs, and defeated the Acolhua. As a result, Azcapotzalco received Texcoco as a tributary. At the beginning of the 15th century, the Tepanec king died. The city fell into civil war with the emergence of two potential rulers. The Mexica preferred Tayahauh, who had been initially enthroned, but his son, Maxtla, usurped power from under him. Maxtla was angered by the fact that the Mexica had not supported him, so he turned on them. He then declared war against the Acolhua as well. The Texcoco king fled and started to look for reinforcements. He received help from the city of Huexotzinco in Puebla and the city of Tlacopan on the western shore of Lake Texcoco. Tenochtitlan joined hands with Texcoco, Tlacopan, and Huexotzinco and engaged in the war against Azcapotzalco. Warfare in Mexico had a somewhat eccentric approach in that they focused on capturing enemies alive for rituals and sacrifices. In 1428, the union of the four cities emerged victoriously.

After the war, Tenochtitlan, Texcoco, and Tlacopan formed an alliance that would commemorate the beginning of the Aztec empire – known today as the Triple Alliance. The spoils of war were distributed among the three cities, with two-fifth of the land going to Tenochtitlan, another two-fifth going to Texcoco, and one-fifth going to Tlacopan. The son of Tezozomoc assumed the position of the ruler in Tlacopan. Tlacopan remained a minor player in the alliance. On the other hand, Texcoco was a dazzling city that fully profited from the tributes. At the time, it was famous for its huge libraries with numerous texts from older Mesoamerican cultures. At its peak, it probably had a population of more than 24,000. Today, it is located in the greater metropolitan area of the Mexican capital, Mexico City. For a brief period in the late 1820s, Texcoco served as the capital of Mexico.

Tenochtitlan became the capital of the Aztec Empire. After allying, the three cities comprising the Aztec Empire became the collective superpower of the region and took control of central Mexico. They continued to exert their power over the Mesoamerican landscape until the arrival of the Spanish. The most significant reason for the Aztecs' loss to the Europeans was the diseases of the Old World. The Mesoamericans succumbed to the oncoming illnesses because their immune systems had evolved differently from the immune system of the invaders.

And, just like that, the Aztec Empire was no more.

The average Joe is liable to mix up different Mesoamerican civilizations. Most of them share major similarities, so it is easy to mistake one for the other. They were mostly tribal cultures with polytheistic beliefs. They were often nomadic and did not mind packing up and leaving a site once it had started to decline. They were often at war with one another, they practiced bloodletting, human sacrifices, and often held public processions and ceremonies. Almost all major Mesoamerican civilizations took an interest in cosmology and the movement of celestial bodies, using a calendar to keep track of their movement. Almost all of them had a writing system, either rudimentary or advanced. Often people get confused by the different cultures. One must ask the question: Aside from their timelines, what is the difference between the Maya, the Aztecs, and other Mesoamerican cultures?

The Maya was a combination of tribes that had settled in southern Mexico and northern Central America and spoke different languages that are termed collectively as Mayan languages. On the other hand, the Aztecs lived in Central Mexico and, for the most part, spoke the

Nahuatl language across the board. In between these two civilizations are the mysterious Toltecs, who act as a connecting paragraph in the annals of history.

PART 3: THE TOLTEC LEGACY: SOCIETY, ARTS, AND CULTURE

Chapter 11: Social Structure

When the Spanish conquest of the Aztecs happened, Nahuatl-speaking groups were widespread all over Mesoamerica. These groups had arrived from the north and had settled in the Valley of Mexico. Most of these groups were unique and diverse, and their languages were variants of each other. Despite the minor linguistic differences, these tribes had the same cultural blueprint. One can notice the similarities in Mesoamerican civilizations throughout history, but these similarities were intensified in the Late Classic and Postclassic Periods, courtesy of the Nahua people who started to arrive in central Mexico. As these people started to work together to form large urban communities, a way of life started to appear that would continue up until the Colonial Period and, to some extent, continues to this day.

Some historians think that the Toltecs arrived in central Mexico as a distinct ethnic group from the deserts in the northwest, stopped at Culhuacan - their first urban city -, and then settled in Tollan. Others believe they were simply urbanized folk as opposed to the ubiquitous barbarians, i.e., the Chichimecs. The beginning of urbanized living, first in Teotihuacán and then in Tula, changed the landscape of the entire region. Large communes started to form that helped each other grow. The trend towards socialization did have its share of issues.

Having no prior experience, most Mesoamerican civilizations, including the Toltecs, fell prey to quite similar troubles.

The biggest issue was the establishment of a class structure that relegated a select few to the comforts and luxuries that were unavailable to the rest. This discrepancy in resource availability is apparent in the Toltec Empire. The Toltec civilization was largely a military aristocracy – the respected military force was full of fearsome and menacing warriors of unmatched resilience. The soldiers were responsible for maintaining the peace and upholding the covenants of law and order. The higher echelons of society consisted of military leaders, priests, and sometimes even merchants and artisans.

During their initial nomadic days, the Toltecs maintained their lifestyle by roaming around the land and locating settlements from whom they would demand tributes after taking over. They would take over one village or city, convert its inhabitants into loyal tributaries, and head over to the next settlement. Despite the back-and-forth skirmishes between different groups, this warriors-taking-tribute approach was novel for its time. The constant clashes had shaped their image as warriors, but there was one major problem: Teotihuacán. The power and influence of Teotihuacán across Mesoamerica were unprecedented for its time, and the city often threw a wrench in the Toltecs' plans. As long as the capital city lasted, it was hard to go against it or its allies. Once Teotihuacán fell, and its commercial networks fell·into disarray, the Toltecs picked the villages apart one by one. Some believe that even the burning of Teotihuacán happened at the hands of the Toltecs. Some sources cite that Mixcoatl led the most significant military campaigns towards the Valley of Mexico.

When they discovered Tula and settled there, the population was already brimming with warriors. Most of the military was used to exert power over the small towns, states, and dominions around central Mexico. This was necessary to continue with their habit of collecting tributes from other states. The tributes that arrived from other groups usually found their way into the treasury or the purses of the aristocracy, but sometimes, the aristocrats would distribute their wealth among the lower classes of their group. The Triple Alliance of the Aztecs adopted the same model. The aristocrats also collected tributes from their local vassals.

Mesoamerican tribes were almost exclusively devout and staunch in their religious beliefs. The Toltecs were no exception. Religion played a crucial role in the normal functioning of society. It had evolved beyond faith and had embedded itself into the social fabric. It was so endemic among the tribes of Mexico that it almost seemed like a universal law. Political and military decisions were taken based on religious ideologies. Sacrificial rituals were performed to appease the gods so that they would grant victory to their followers. This deep-seated belief in their pantheon of gods allowed the Toltecs to persevere over the centuries. Even in their early days, there were extremely cautious of which way their gods were leaning to avoid vexing them. The Toltec religion was shamanic, and people often conducted religious practices without strict adherence to a specific place or building. They had pantheistic beliefs, so they thought that the natural forces of the world were manifestations of a higher power. They worshipped water, earth, and sun, and as such, the location was not of paramount importance. With the advent of urbanization, they got more comfortable with processions and social rituals. The Mesoamerican ball game was the biggest example of their religious beliefs. Some historians think that the winners were sacrificed as a way of spiritual vindication and exaltation. Others believe that the losers were sacrificed to the gods, essentially killing two birds with one stone.

Eventually, the first king was crowned who, as discussed earlier, could have been one of many potential figures. The king was the leader of the physical as well as spiritual realms. He would often keep the military class very close since the commerce of the Empire depended on it. The priests were important for conducting religious ceremonies and advising the public in spiritual and social situations.

The nobles and religious leaders wore jewelry and donned bright attires. The military had a uniform, but the prestigious heroes would wear lavish clothes with lots of jewelry. Some people think that the Toltec nobility might have kept slaves as well, but the evidence for this is quite circumstantial. Proponents of this theory say that the Toltecs can be seen dragging weeping individuals from the Huastec tribe in some drawings. However, these people could easily have been on their way to a sacrificial ceremony.

Under the upper class of the military and priests, there was probably a middle class of artists, merchants, astronomers, sculptors, and other skilled workers. This demographic may not have enjoyed the liberties of the elites, but they were, by and large, sophisticated people who spent a healthy life and received social benefits. The commoners were builders involved in the construction of monuments or farmers who worked in the outskirts of the cities. They did not possess the honor or stature of the nobles. As opposed to the vibrant attires of the aristocrats, the commoners wore a simple loincloth and a Tilma, known in Nahuatl as "tilmàtli." The commoners did not belong to the Toltec bloodline – or in many cases, the fabricated royal bloodline – and would probably have come from other groups or vassal states. The elites held almost all major designations in government. They enforced restrictions so that no commoner could reach a major rank in the army or priesthood. The most exceptional commoners who had displayed feats of strength and wisdom were welcomed into the government, albeit in offices of lesser value.

Agriculture may have been central to the Toltec economy, but there are major issues in ascertaining whether their agricultural produce was cultivated locally or imported from other places as a form of tribute. Should the latter be true, the probability of slavery in the Postclassic Era increases. According to most estimates, maize, beans, and chili peppers were cultivated around Tula, whereas cacao and mushrooms were imported. Most of the cultivation was done using the technique of hill terracing. Their irrigation systems, although not exemplary, were better than most Mesoamerican civilizations. The Toltecs extracted different parts of corn vegetation for medicinal and ornamental purposes, used cotton for weaving clothes, and used the maguey plant for fermenting alcoholic drinks. The land of Tula was probably fertile in the Postclassic Period, but during the occasional famine or drought, the Toltecs harvested and consumed amaranth. As far as trade is concerned, we know that textiles and ceramics were exported from Tula, and jade, turquoise, obsidian, exotic bird, and animal skins made their way into the city. The Toltecs were adept at establishing monopolies and forbade the bartering of rare goods to other cultures. They also knew when to increase and decrease prices according to the supply and demand of an item.

The Maya used to conduct extensive trade throughout the region, and with the emergence of Teotihuacán, more routes started to pop up. This vast existing network helped the Toltecs launch their trade. Archaeologists have uncovered pottery from Nicaragua, Costa Rica, and Guatemala in Tula, proving that the Toltecs conducted trade over long distances. Some ceramic material from Veracruz has also been found at Tula. Moreover, Tula was involved in the production of pottery, bowls, and items made from obsidian. It is not known whether Tula was directly involved in the production of these goods or a nearby area produced them under the directions of Tula.

The expansion of trade and territory using staunch religious ideology might have proved costly for the Toltecs in the long run. Some people credit their strict adherence to war-like ways for their eventual demise. The Toltecs expanded at an exponential pace throughout Mesoamerica based on violence. This makes historians wonder if they were sharp enough to take full advantage of their political and economic circumstances. Some theorists think that the Gulf Coast might have been at the forefront of trade in Mesoamerica instead of Tollan.

The rapid expansion of the empire did not allow the multiple ethnicities of the empire to integrate peacefully. There is plenty of room for error when a multi-ethnic empire has numerous vassal states of a diverse ethnic makeup under its rule. These issues might have been integral in igniting the constant civil wars between the cults of Quetzalcoatl and Tezcatlipoca. The battles with the Otomi and the Huastec people may have also been the result of rapid expansion and lack of cohesion between the different factions of society.

A lot of literature discusses the possibility of the Toltecs being several groups of Nahuatl-speaking people that did not constitute an "empire." The people who prefer this position think that these groups had overlapping similarities and formed cultural hybrids with other groups and cultures. Consequently, the Toltecs of Tula were somewhat different from the Toltecs of Chichen Itza, who, in turn, were quite different from the Toltec Maya, and so on. They point out that the terms Toltec and Tollan could have referred to more than four particular groups and four different states, respectively. The variations of the Toltecs include the group at Tula de Allende, the Toltec-Maya who inhabited Chichen Itza, the inhabitants of Teotihuacán and its surroundings, and the ethnic group Tolteca Chichimeca. These various possible versions of the Toltecs had differences in their social conduct, but if one were to paint with a broad stroke, it would be hard to discern the differences. Because of the similarities in social conduct, religion, and origins of all these groups, it is hard to distinguish between them unless someone stumbles upon major discoveries in the future. Not only that, but the evolution of all groups also followed similar trajectories when they shifted from agrarian communes to urban states.

Normally, we associate rural life with a free and uninhibited lifestyle with little to no social contact. Its appreciation depends on one's sensitivity towards nature. However, in the case of ancient civilization, this was often not the case. Agricultural lifestyles endorsed tribalism and served as a breeding ground for false notions of tribal superiority and ethnic dominance. Loyalty to the tribe would often become a source of egotism and eventually give rise to greed and lust for power. Most Mesoamerican tribes were nomadic, which means that they were almost always on the move. They rarely had time to settle down and make time for civilized progression. Every activity was geared towards short-term survival. This behavior is quite common in the animal kingdom. Fortunately, man learns to socialize. Gradually, he starts to understand that inter-community and intra-community relations are not always a zero-sum game. Many occasions call for communication, and acting on these opportunities often leads to a rewarding outcome for all parties involved. Tribalism had always prevailed in Mesoamerica, which is why the development of Teotihuacán and the ensuing Toltec Empire were life-altering revelations for the locals.

Chapter 12: Arts, Sculpture, and Architecture

The Toltecs were master artisans, sculptures, and architects. They were revered throughout the land for their decorations of pottery, ornaments, jewelry, stonemasonry, and buildings. It is no wonder that the word, Toltec, became synonymous with the word, artist, in Mesoamerican lands. These praises were certainly warranted, as anyone can gather from the remains of Tula. One must remember that Tula was destroyed and burned, so what we see on the site today might be a very small area within the larger premises of the original city.

Tula and other Toltec territories were raided and looted after the demise of their empire. Aztecs, who held them in high regard, would often take relics, valuables, and stone carvings while passing through lands of the former empire. Archaeological research dictates that the Aztecs took relics from Teotihuacán as well. The Spanish invasions took care of the rest. As far as we know, the Spanish burnt written codices of the Toltecs without exception - pending discovery. The Spanish did the same to the Maya and Aztec codices, too, but somehow, some documents have survived. Some post-conquest codices were also compiled to transcribe the history of the Aztecs and the Maya. In the Colonial Era, priceless artwork was looted and sold on the black market. Unfortunately, for these reasons, most Toltec art has been lost to the annals of history, unlike most Mayan and Aztec artifacts that have survived to date. Even the sculptures of ancient Olmec have survived the brunt of time. In the case of the Toltecs, the most significant pieces of their legacy include the collective site of Tula Chico and Tula Grande and an obsidian workshop near Tula. However, enough of it has survived to serve as a testament to their majestic prowess in the arts. Their emergence had such a distinct impact on areas in the north of Mexico and central Mexico that civilizations in those areas witnessed a rejuvenation of spirit. The Huastec in the north and the Tarascos in the west are witnesses to this adventurous fervor. From this period onwards, these cultures started to develop lasting architectural and sculptural statements.

The Classic Period in Mesoamerica saw the apex of Mayan creativity. Some even believe that it was as relevant for the region as Renaissance was for Europe. Most of these Maya contributions show Mexican values, hinting at a Toltec-Maya collaboration. We know that these Mexican values infiltrated not just central Mexico but southern Mexico and northern parts of Central America as well. In Chichen Itza, we see the themes of Toltec art develop in tandem with Tula. Eagles and jaguars devour human hearts, and gathered skulls are placed on altars called "tzompantli." Tzompantli had a scaffold-like construction of poles and was found in several Mesoamerican civilizations, including the Maya and the Aztec cities. The skulls normally belonged to sacrificial victims and war captives. The tzompantli at Tula has rows of stone carvings on the sides of a broad platform that depict the skulls of the sacrificial victims. The real skulls of the victims were displayed on these platforms. In Chichen Itza, the tzompantli appears on the sidewalls of the ballcourt. Other Maya cities like Uxmal also have some examples of the ancient device. This practice probably appeared in Tula in the late stages, shortly before its fall. The Aztecs continued the tradition, and a tzompantli still exists in Tenochtitlan. There were at least five more tzompantli in the Aztec capital city when the Spanish arrived. In different Aztec codices, we can see the tzompantli depicted in the context of ballgames.

Looking at Toltec art, one instantly reaches the same conclusion that one reaches when looking at works from the High Renaissance: It was a cultural phenomenon that pervaded multiple cities, a mode of conversation – not just between different minds but also between different lifestyles and social values. The one thing that unites almost all Toltec art is the consistent use of religious motifs. This religious current permeated every aspect of their lives.

These people were not privy to the Greek revolution of reason and logic, so they regaled themselves with myths and fables that seeped into the sociological framework. One watches in awe as the warriors and priests perform their duties, and the gods go about their divine work in the images. The events exaggerated, the figures elevated to heroes, these works of art are, first and foremost, dramatic works. For instance, the relief at Building 4 in Tula shows a procession heading towards a man dressed as a feathered serpent. Some believe that the Atlantean statues at the heart of the city were not depictions of the average Toltec warrior but a representation of Tlahuizcalpantecuhtli – the god of the morning star who was one of the many forms of Quetzalcoatl – or his followers.

The Atlantean sculptures are among the finest examples of Toltec art. Carrying a curved weapon, darts, and knives, these figures are renowned for their solemn devotion and grand scale. This sentiment extends itself to the smaller ceramic and stone figurines as well as relief and stone carvings. Most of what we know about Toltec art comes from these figures since the stone at the site of Tula has persevered against the hardships of climate and time. The signature sculpture of perhaps the entire Toltec civilization is the reclining figure of a man. Known as "chacmool," these figures represent male warriors facing 90 degrees from the front, supporting themselves on their elbows and knees and carrying a bowl or a disc in their lap. For the most part, the chacmools portrayed slain soldiers who were carrying offerings to the gods. The receptacle in the middle of the sculpture carries alcoholic drink, tortilla, tamale, turkey, feathers, tobacco, or incense. The 12 chacmools in Tula have standardized features and are quite similar except for some minor changes. It is quite probable that the ones in Tula represent war captives. As the influence of the Toltecs grew, chacmools started to appear all over Mesoamerica. They started appearing in the Yucatán and even as far away as Costa Rica. The chacmools at Chichen Itza are not all similar and vary somewhat in their features. The Aztec chacmools have an association with water and are often linked with the god of rain.

Toltec art is also credited with the introduction of plumbate – a distinct style of glazed pottery that uses metals like copper, silver, and gold. Usually associated with the use of a special type of clay, it was one of the most unique artistic statements of its time, evolving because of Toltec ingenuity. The Toltecs were known for their orange-colored and dark-colored plumbate pottery with a glossy exterior full of incised decoration, portraying a variety of styles. The Toltecs also perfected the inlays in turquoise and other materials. Around this time, archaeologists notice the appearance of metals throughout Mesoamerica. Metals like gold and silver started being used for creating different items, probably popularized by their use as metallic gleams in plumbate.

The motifs from sculpture appear in different structures throughout the city architecture as well. The architecture of the Toltecs is exemplary for its time. The Toltecs derived most of their architectural influences from Teotihuacán but added freshness, character, and nuance to them. The city square of Tula is largely reminiscent of the one at Teotihuacán, both in design and pattern. The Pyramid C at Tula has the same astronomical orientation as the Aztec city. Despite the influence, Toltec art evolves heavily from the basic premise. At the time, no civilization was designing cities based on grid plans - Teotihuacán first popularized the idea – but most of Tula was designed according to a grid plan. At its peak, it had a population of 85,000 that was creatively spread out throughout the city's central districts and outskirts. At least 60,000 people lived inside the city and 25,000 right outside of it. Granted, the peak population of Tula was much smaller than other Mesoamerican metropolitans, but it was the biggest Mesoamerican city of its era. The structures were made from stone, and then an adobe finish was applied to them. The pyramids, palaces, and other royal buildings had relief sculptures and friezes on the fringes. Tula has a ton of relief sculptures and friezes, including the Wall of Serpents that has elaborate carvings of snakes devouring human beings as well as geometric designs. The wall separated the sacred precinct from the rest of the city.

The people who lived in the city lived in large apartment complexes. Most of them would have been aristocrats or belonged to the middle class. The city also had palaces and group homes. The city was divided into districts: people from different backgrounds and socio-economic standing would have lived in different neighborhoods. The smaller classes outside the city would probably have lived in houses made of lower-grade materials, making them susceptible to environmental damage. They have probably perished after years of perpetual damage.

Several houses may have perished, and great monuments may have been burned, but fortunately, archaeologists have found thousands of pieces of pottery at Tula. Some of these items were locally produced, while others were brought there from far away; some of them are in great shape, while others are partially damaged. Experts think that Tula's brand of plumbate pottery was unique and original. The Aztecs were adamant that the Toltecs had refined the art of clay. Excavations have revealed that the Toltecs made Mazapan-style ceramics for themselves and brought other styles of pottery from foreign lands as tribute or imports. The local potters were also adept at creating pottery pieces with faces. Not only that, but the Toltecs also made nose rings, earplugs, and other forms of jewelry using jade, turquoise, and gold.

Near the end of the 10th century, the western region of Mexico saw an uptick in creative zeal and vigor. Up until that point, they had carried minor influences from the Olmecs and the artisans of Teotihuacán. Incorporating the Toltec influence, they started creating exquisite items of gold and silver, as well as polychrome vessels. This rebirth was not restricted to small-scale arts but extended to architecture as well. During this period, the Tarascan region began erecting buildings using stone. Tzintzuntzan, meaning "place of hummingbirds," the ceremonial center at the Tarascan state capital is the prime example of this change. Here we find the Yacatas, five rounded pyramids that stand atop a large platform. At the summit of the pyramids, there were wooden temples for performing sacred rites. Just like the western areas of Mexico, the northern areas were highly influenced by the artistic endeavors in central Mexico – exemplified by the case of La Quemada. The tribes that constituted the Aztec Empire originated from the north, and that region was home to nomadic people. The people there became more and more interested in small-scale arts like sculpture and pottery. For instance, in Casas Grandes, people produced intricate pottery designs based on geometric patterns.

The Toltecs may have made their name because of their military prowess, but they were just as talented in the artistic department. With great experiences comes the need for expression. What we see with the evolution of arts in Toltec society is not unusual. It is a perfectly sound response to the whims of the time. The ancient world was nowhere as fixated on the global perspective as the modern world. They did not have the luxury to travel distances as tourists and engage with other cultures. The Toltecs were nomadic, so they would often encounter other groups and had a militaristic approach to politics, which kept them in contact with those groups. For the ancient Mesoamerican world, this kind of exposure was extremely exciting. With the tributes pouring in to Tula and the newfound activity on trade routes, people were coming in touch with different perspectives and novel ideas. The most common example of this is the mysterious connection between Tula and Chichen Itza.

The Toltec influence of arts took over the entire Mesoamerican land, and even their fall from grace could not hamper the pace of this expansion. In times like these, art becomes a sort of conversation, a back-and-forth between different artists living in the same landscape and somewhat similar conditions. The artistic genius of the Toltecs and its impact in Mesoamerica is undeniable. Coming into power in the Late Classic Era and taking over the collective subconscious of the entire region in the Postclassic Era, the Toltecs have certainly left their mark in the pre-Columbian history of the New World. We may not fully understand them, but we know how they felt.

Chapter 13: Warfare and Weaponry

Finally, we arrive at the central pillar of Toltec life, the tenet that helped them build their empire and prosper as a people: *Warfare*.

Mesoamerican cultures upheld priests as the highest authority. The Toltecs were the first Mesoamerican society where the military was showered with the same prestige and status as priests. They elevated warfare from the needless clashes and skirmishes based on hate and fearmongering – and turned it into a viable source of income. When they left the northwestern deserts and arrived in central Mexico, they battered and bullied other groups into submission, quickly carving out their space in the harsh landscape. They opposed the idea of bloodshed and useless killing and would often take war captives to serve the needs of the group at large. These needs fluctuated between economic and spiritual. They would often need other groups to send them tribute, and when they took prisoners, they would put them to work or offer them to the gods.

Historical data regarding their vassal states is limited, but we know that the Toltecs held some states in central Mexico as vassals and demanded the tribute of food, goods, weapons, and soldiers. Historians are divided regarding the scope of this exercise. Some believe that it may have reached the Gulf Coast. Whether it was to and from trade with the Gulf Coast or a one-way journey of tribute is unknown. As far as solid, conclusive evidence is concerned, we rarely come across it when dealing with the Toltecs. There is no definitive evidence that the Toltecs held sway over any state more than 1000 kilometers away from Tula. We notice the socio-political influence of Toltec art all over the region, but that does not speak to the extent of the Toltec empire. Historians mostly believe that while the Toltecs probably held military influence over their neighboring areas, their influences in far-off regions can be attributed to trade or exile groups.

The Toltecs developed a military mindset from a young age. Those who wished to master Toltec knowledge would often study in telpochcalli and then in calmécaca – these were centers for education, and here, they would gain their basic understanding of the spiritual war. The intense religious perspective of the world helped them realize the transient and ephemeral nature of life. Such an understanding was crucial to weed out resistance, cowardice, and fear from the minds and hearts of the disciples. The men and women who partook in the activities at these institutions were known as warriors. They would learn to deceive their ego, control their impulses, stonewall the material inertia of the world, and allow harmony and peace into their inner sanctum. In some ways, the Toltec understanding of the world paralleled the teachings of Buddhism, but that is a discussion for another time.

The warriors were taught to look for their one true aim: their purpose in life. The object of the training was to help them reveal their personalities to themselves. The rest was not of any consequence – his iron will and determination would see to it that his mission was achieved. The possibilities of the spirit were endless, and so, worldly achievements were never beyond the realm of possibility. The idea was that the few basic forces that control the world manifested themselves in different physical manners, so if one could harness the spiritual force of the self, he could fulfill his purpose in the vast cosmology of events.

To enforce this understanding, the Toltecs had military orders, including but not restricted to the eagle, the coyote, and the jaguar. Some people like to refer to these religious warrior orders as cults. Excavations have revealed a small statue of a Tlaloc warrior cult in a ballcourt in Tula. Such statues have also been found at Teotihuacán. As discussed briefly in an earlier chapter, some people thought that the Atlantean statues might have been divine or semi-divine figures. They are adorned with the symbols of Quetzalcoatl that depict them as servants of the god. This may be in part due to the Toltec warrior's allegiance to a particular warrior cult. Think back to the cults of Tezcatlipoca and Quetzalcoatl, who went head-to-head against each other in a battle for supremacy. After Topiltzin left Tollan, the Toltecs chose Huitzilopochtli as their patron. If you don't recall, Huitzilopochtli was the Nahua god of war. He was worshipped by the Mexica and was the patron deity of Tenochtitlan.

The language of ancient Mesoamerica was often quite poetic. Things were not elaborated by pale descriptions. The concepts of the spirit were relayed with the power of abstraction. Metaphors were used to engage with the reader on an intuitive level. The great philosophers were not master of reason; they were masters of language. For explaining the concept of the warrior, their metaphoric language uses the words "flower" and "song." The Toltecs believed that wisdom was full of inherent beauty, and the embodiment of this beauty could only be achieved by the expression of the spirit. So, beauty was the proverbial garden where the songs, the flowers of wisdom, grew. As mentioned earlier, students of higher education were known as warriors, and most of them would serve as members of the military force. With the beautiful use of language, the Toltecs emphasized that a great warrior was the one who was sensitive to the order of things, responsible to his purpose, and disciplined in his execution.

The warrior's sensitivity kept him for killing for the sake of killing. He or she would refrain from conflict unless it was called for. By becoming conscious of the world and its inhabitants, he realized that they are self-aware beings as well. Some may delve into the conscious abstractions of the world more than others, but everyone exhibits awareness of other beings and the world around them. To avail them of their lives for the cultivation of one's ego would be an egregious sin and a loss for one's soul. Responsibility defers one, once again, to the order of things. A single human being does not inhabit the world. People live, they die, others take their place, everyone is equally helpless before nature. Therefore, the warrior was called upon to realize his responsibility – not just to himself but also to the natural world at large. He could not give in to pride or greed, he could not be fixated on the follies of the world, and he should only have been loyal to his ultimate aim in the world – the ambition of his spirit. This sense of responsibility distinguished the warrior from the average Joe in the street. The warrior had the responsibility to manifest his wisdom and knowledge by the power of action. The third tenet, discipline, was the willpower to execute said action. The Toltec warriors had a completely different understanding of discipline than the one often preached in the modern world. For the Toltecs, discipline was a personal regime and did not belong to a group or a political cause. Although it could have only belonged to the warrior, it needed to be cultivated. His will and resolve were tested to see whether he was up to the task. If the spirit were pure, it would get the body to fulfill its spiritual responsibility. To achieve discipline, he had to be sensitive towards the inner and outer workings of the world and had to know his responsibility to both. Only then, it was believed, could he master the art of discipline. This mindset was quite humbling for the warrior. Its goal was to turn warriors into solemn beings, very much like the priests who governed high society.

The Quetzalcoatl was the ultimate expression of this ideal. The feathered serpent slithered on the earth, touched it, and learned its secrets. When it was time, the quetzal – the sacred bird – spread its wings and left the earth in search of a new path among the clouds. Quetzalcoatl symbolized the importance of the other planes of existence and removed emphasis from the one the warriors saw, heard, and breathed in. All these ideas can be found in the Cantares Mexicanos, a Nahuatl manuscript from the 16th century that contains poems and songs. Historical data indicates that the realization of all these ideals was not always possible. Things would often spiral out of control, descending the city of Tula into turmoil and chaos. The warrior cults would go against each other, as demonstrated by the cults of Quetzalcoatl and Tezcatlipoca.

Skilled, terrifying, and highly trained, the Toltecs had a standing army in their states and garrisons in other states as well. The standing army would defend against foes, whereas the foreign legions would keep the vassal states in check and protect them from outside interference. They also had reserve units in the cities that they could call upon in times of need. The neighboring states were not in awe of the Toltecs because of their skills on the battlefield. They respected them for building a system that incorporated military values so aptly into the everyday life of an urban environment. For instance, Tula did not have any heavy defenses incorporated into the city design. Bear in mind that Tula had a grid plan, so they must have had time to work out the needs of the city. The Toltecs were confident in their ability to protect the city from outsiders, no matter what.

The Toltec warriors can be seen in different statues, friezes, stelae, and other works of art found at Tula and other sites. For protection, they wore decorative chest plates and cotton armors that were heavily padded to deflect oncoming arrows and spears. The breastplate would often have an image of a jaguar, a coyote, or an eagle to distinguish the warrior's cult. A short kilt was worn to protect the lower half of the torso. Their helmets were adorned with feathers, and they used sandals and straps to obscure legs and ankles, but these would have provided little in the way of protection. They preferred small, round shields because they wrapped one arm from the shoulder down in padding. An armored tunic was uncovered in the Burned Palace of Tula. Made of seashells, this elegant and well-crafted armor probably belonged to a high-level officer or a member of the nobility. Their choice of weapons was rather interesting. They liked to use swords, maces, knives, and curved clubs with blades for close-range combat, fastening them with a belt. For ranged combat, they employed atlatls, which launches spears or javelins. They would use it to shoot long darts with remarkable precision.

The true genius of the Toltecs lay not in teaching their warriors to effectively yield a sword but in managing the psychological and sociological aspects associated with military service. Their unshaken trust in their abilities and the depth of their tactical and strategic ventures were more than enough to strike fear in the hearts of their enemies. By extracting students of higher education, they were able to bring the cream of the crop to the military. However, this practice also proved to be their downfall. No matter how well-educated and well-disciplined a military force is, it will always succumb to greed, lust, and agendas of power. Such is the nature of the work – engaging in battles, thriving in tough situations, and priding yourself on the toughness of competition are all actions that induce adrenaline. It is quite easy to succumb to it, which is why military regimes throughout history have had a hard time keeping up with the needs of the state.

It is possible that natural disasters, instead of the unusual social structure, wiped the Toltec empire from the face of the Earth – just as they believed: everything is ephemeral, and change is the only constant. Civilizations rise, and civilizations fall. Sometimes, it takes centuries; sometimes, it takes years. But the demise is inevitable. After all, whatever goes up must come down. Unfortunately, for the Toltecs, the fall came like a bolt of lightning.

Conclusion

In the Classic Period of Mesoamerican civilization, the Maya entered their golden age. During this time, the Maya erected monuments based on the calculations of their Long Count calendar. As they opted for large-scale construction, they ushered in a new era in the history of the region. The innovation and the ambitious outlook of the lowland Maya inspired their neighbors. The Maya wrote inscriptions, integrated calendars into their daily lives, and emphasized artistic and intellectual development. A wave of urbanism followed. Art historians have likened the Classic Maya's influence to that of the Renaissance in Europe. As the Maya shifted from a purely agrarian culture to an urban lifestyle, they started to form small city-states. These states quickly began interacting with each other, forming alliances, forging trade routes, and navigating a competitive environment.

At the same time, a religious center emerged in the Mexican Highlands, known as "Teotihuacán." What began as a ceremonial site soon started to attract migrants from all over the region. The city witnessed an influx of the Zapotec, the Mixtec, and the Maya people, turning it into a multi-ethnic state. In a short time, the city developed its reputation as the most extravagant city of Mesoamerica and started to exert its influence on its neighbors, including the Maya. In the Late Classic Period, famine and drought took over the land, and the unforgiving climate made it difficult to survive in the city. The city was eventually burnt and looted – probably due to internal strife –, and a hefty majority of the population migrated to the surrounding areas. After the fall of Teotihuacán, the Maya started to witness some internal issues as well. The states of Tikal and Calakmul went to war. After a long back-and-forth, the Maya were weakened. Teotihuacán was proof that a metropolitan city could be established in the region.

In the Late and Terminal Classic Periods, some nomadic groups started arriving in Central Mexico from the north. Some of these tribes settled on the site of Tula and gave birth to the Toltec Empire. Some people think that the Toltecs had been living there for a few centuries and were even involved in the destruction of Teotihuacán. Others believe that they arrived shortly after the fall of Teotihuacán and imbued the land with an aura of wisdom and fear.

So, who were the Toltecs? Where did they come from? Where did they go?

Nobody knows. All we have is the art of speculation. Presumably, they migrated from the north, settled at Culhuacan, and finally arrived at Tula. In Tula, the Toltecs were ruled by the mesmerizing figure of Cē Ācatl Topiltzin, also known as "Quetzalcoatl." The feathered serpent educated them, teaching them how to grow crops, read a calendar, and engage with the spiritual essence of the self. Like most Mesoamerican cultures, the Toltecs were religious people who practiced human sacrifice and bloodletting.

The Toltecs had a military-based society where warriors were groomed from a young age. They were the first civilization in Mesoamerica that turned its combat skills into a viable source of income. Their military conquests were backed by their religious foundations. They took over the city-states of the region and demanded tributes from them. Units were sent to vassal states to maintain peace and receive regular tributes. The Toltecs had a fondness for warrior cults, and excavations reveal that warriors belonged to orders of jaguars, coyotes, and eagles. These cults had specific religious ideologies and were responsible for the biggest divide in Toltec society. Some supported the cult of Quetzalcoatl, whereas others supported the cult of Tezcatlipoca. In some ways, the religious ambitions of the two cults were opposite to each other.

Cē Ācatl Topiltzin Quetzalcoatl was renowned for his humanist ideals. He abolished the Mesoamerican tradition of human sacrifice and only offered foods and animals to the gods. The insight of Topiltzin helped Tula thrive and prosper for years. One day, Tezcatlipoca appeared before him as an old man and tricked him. After being humiliated, Quetzalcoatl left the city and headed east. When he reached the shore, he burnt himself on a pyre and turned into a star – to return in the future. This, of course, is the mythological version of the story as told by the Aztecs. After the self-imposed exile of Topiltzin, Tula was razed and burnt to the ground. Many people believe that the cults probably went to war against one another, and Tezcatlipoca emerged victoriously. Some refute that statement and claim that natural disasters caused famine, hunger, and disease, forcing people to flee. Theorists like to speculate, but the fact of the matter is that *nobody knows what happened.*

The cult of Quetzalcoatl did spread throughout the region. For instance, it is known that there was some mysterious connection between the city of Tula and the Maya city, Chichen Itza. The Temple of Quetzalcoatl in Chichen Iza, also known as "El Castillo," depicts the shadow of a serpent on the equinoxes. Moreover, one finds many drawings and inscriptions of the feathered serpent in Uxmal. Even though the image of the feathered serpent existed in the Preclassic Era, Quetzalcoatl did not appear until the Late Classic Era.

The cult of Quetzalcoatl permeated the land of central Mexico. The Aztecs added him to the pantheon of their gods and held him in high esteem. They revered the Toltecs so much that they claimed to have descended from them. It was common practice to claim Toltec descent to get recognized as nobles, making it extremely difficult for historians to differentiate between the historical figure, Topiltzin, and the god, Quetzalcoatl. The cult of Quetzalcoatl was a widely held belief among the Aztecs. It is said that when Hernan Cortes invaded Mesoamerica, the Aztec king, Montezuma, mistook him for the reincarnation of Quetzalcoatl.

In addition to being great warriors, the Toltecs were also great artists. The Aztecs were in awe of their scientific and artistic achievements. The Toltecs developed their style of pottery called plumbate pottery. They were responsible for popularizing metalwork in Mesoamerica. They used jade, silver, obsidian, gold, and copper to create pottery, jewelry, and other items. They also made major contributions to the fields of sculpture and architecture. The Atlantean statues standing in the middle of Tula are fine examples of their talent and skill. The Toltecs were also responsible for introducing large-scale terraced agriculture and high-quality ceramics.

The Toltecs introduced a new political system in Mesoamerica: militarism. It became the norm for various empires in the Terminal Classic and Postclassic Periods, including the Aztecs. The Aztec Empire, an alliance of three states, sustained itself by collecting tributes from its vassals. The Toltecs are the missing part of the story – the invisible link that joins the Maya and Teotihuacán to the Aztec Empire. We may not know who they were, where they came from, or how they disappeared, but their contributions to world heritage stand as proof of their undeniable genius.

Here's another book by Enthralling History that you might be interested in

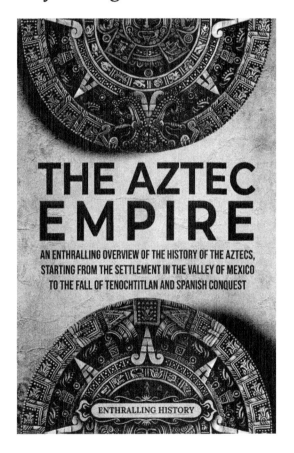

Free limited time bonus

Stop for a moment. We have a free bonus set up for you. The problem is this: we forget 90% of everything that we read after 7 days. Crazy fact, right? Here's the solution: we've created a printable, 1-page pdf summary for this book that you're reading now. All you have to do to get your free pdf summary is to go to the following website:

https://livetolearn.lpages.co/enthrallinghistory/

Once you do, it will be intuitive. Enjoy, and thank you!

We forget 90% of everything that we've read in 7 days...

Get the free printable pdf summary of the book you've read AND much, much more... shhhh...

Enter Your Most Frequently Used Email to Get Started

DOWNLOAD FREE PDF SUMMARY

© Enthralling History

Bibliography:

Include the following references at the end of the book:

Nigel Davies. The Toltecs, until the fall of Tula. University of Oklahoma Press; January 1, 1977.

Nigel Davies. The Toltec Heritage: From the Fall of Tula to the Rise of Tenochtitlan. University of Oklahoma Press; January 1, 1980.

Richard A. Diehl. Tula: The Toltec Capital of Ancient Mexico. New York: Thames & Hudson; November 1, 1983.

H. B. Nicholson. Topiltzin Quetzalcoatl: The Once and Future Lord of the Toltecs. University Press of Colorado; September 15, 2001.

Frank Díaz. The Gospel of the Toltecs: The Life and Teachings of Quetzalcoatl. Bear & Company; July 30, 2002.

Jeff Karl Kowalski. Cynthia Kristan-Graham. George J. Bey III. Twin Tollans: Chichén Itzá, Tula, and the Epiclassic to Early Postclassic Mesoamerican World, Revised Edition. Dumbarton Oaks Research Library and Collection; November 28, 2011.

Michael D. Coe, Stephen D. Houston. The Maya (Ancient Peoples and Places). Thames & Hudson; June 16, 2015.

Elliot M. Abrams. How the Maya Built Their World: Energetics and Ancient Architecture. University of Texas Press; June 4, 2010.

Printed in Great Britain
by Amazon

80273598R00068